ADDITIONAL PRAISE FOR

LESSONS FROM A LEMONADE STAND

"*Lessons from a Lemonade Stand* is the book I wish had been available to me when my children were teenagers and were asking me about government, law, and freedom. In a clear and understandable way it explains why the state is a problem for those of us who value freedom, what real law is, as opposed to the fickle and often irrational dictates of so-called "lawmakers," and why our consent to government may not be all that it appears to be on the surface. If you want to know why kids who sell lemonade outside their homes are dangerous law-breakers who must be forcibly restrained lest they cause you irreparable harm, *read this book*!"

—**Gerard Casey**, professor emeritus of philosophy at University College Dublin and author, *Libertarian Anarchy*

"Ever have that gut reaction against a stupid law or bumbling bureaucracy—the incensed feeling that it's just plain wrong? Boyack has your back. He reveals that not only is your gut correct, but that there are principled, logical reasons why. *Lessons from a Lemonade Stand* provides crucial distinctions between what's legal and what's right, states and governments, and obedience versus justice. It also provides a compelling alternative."

—**Isaac Morehouse**, founder of Praxis and author, *Freedom Without Permission*

D1546462

"Connor Boyack has packed a course on law and philosophy into one fascinating read. I couldn't put it down! The premise is fundamental: What is the basis of the law and of individual rights? Yet the examples and cases are so lively and fun I want to share it with everyone, especially my university students. Boyack takes the reader on a journey filled with shocking and hilarious stories through history, with plenty from current news and lots of footnotes for further reading. It is smooth sailing and enjoyable while filled with endless points of discussion covering natural law, common law, statutory law, jury nullification, etc. from the vantage point of Monty Python, Ayn Rand, Frédéric Bastiat, and Lysander Spooner. I'm sending a copy to my daughter today."

—**Ken Schoolland**, Associate Professor of Economics at Hawaii Pacific University and author, *The Adventures of Jonathan Gullible: A Free Market Odyssey*

LESSONS FROM A LEMONADE STAND

AN UNCONVENTIONAL GUIDE TO GOVERNMENT

CONNOR BOYACK

LIBERTAS PRESS
SALT LAKE CITY, UT

Libertas Press
785 East 200 South, Suite 2
Lehi, UT 84043

Lessons from a Lemonade Stand: An Unconventional Guide to
Government — 1st ed.

ISBN-13 978-1-943521-18-0 (paperback)

For bulk orders, send inquiries to info@libertasutah.org.

10 9 8 7 6 5 4 3

Contents

Other titles by the author:

Passion-Driven Education: How to Use Your Child's Interests to Ignite a Lifelong Love of Learning

Feardom: How Politicians Exploit Your Emotions and What You Can Do to Stop Them

The Tuttle Twins children's book series

Anxiously Engaged: Essays on Faith, Family, & Freedom

Latter-day Responsibility: Choosing Liberty through Personal Accountability

Latter-day Liberty: A Gospel Approach to Government and Politics

To Aaron Russo

for being my Morpheus

None are more hopelessly enslaved than those who falsely believe they are free.

—JOHANN WOLFGANG VON GOETHE

INTRODUCTION

If your neighborhood is anything like mine, you often see lemonade stands setting up shop during the warm summer season. They're a great way for children to learn how to run a business and make a sale. And even when siblings drink half of the product or the weather turns cool and cloudy, children are enthralled by the idea of making money in such a fun, refreshing way.

As it turns out, these lemonade stands are often criminal enterprises.

Take the case of Abigail Krutsinger, a four-year-old who decided, with her parents' help, to offer some refreshing drinks to bikers and tourists passing through her small city in Iowa for the annual bicycle ride across the state. After half an hour of selling lemonade at 25 cents per cup, she had made $5—not bad for a girl her age. Then the police arrived and shut her down.

Abigail's crime? She didn't obtain a permit—a government permission slip. Even if she and her family had wanted to obtain this permission, the city was demanding a staggering $400—just to sell some lemonade! Disappointed that his daughter was denied an opportunity to gain experience running a (very) small business, Abigail's father said, "If the line is drawn to the point where a 4-year-old... can't sell a couple glasses of lemonade for 25 cents, then I think the line has been drawn at the wrong spot."[1]

Abigail is not an anomaly. A few teenage girls in Midway, Georgia, built enough of an operation that they named themselves the "Midway Lemonade Girls" and got some corporate sponsors. These girls were trying to earn enough money to visit a nearby water park, but their efforts were thwarted by the city's police chief who, after ending these girls' experience in entrepreneurship, told reporters he "didn't know how the lemonade was made, who made it or what was in it." To obey the law in their city, the girls would have had to pay the city $50 each day for a business and health permit, even if they were operating on their driveway. "It's kind of crazy that we couldn't sell lemonade," said 14-year-old Kasity Dixon, one of the Midway Lemonade Girls. "It was fun, but we had to listen to the cops and shut it down." The police chief, interviewed by a local news station, recalled what his law enforcement officers had told the girls:

> We had told them, "We understand you guys are young, but still, you're breaking the law, and we can't let you do it anymore. The law is the law, and we have to be consistent with how we enforce the laws."[2]

Then there's the case of the Marriott and Augustine kids, whose families joined forces to sell lemonade to the hordes of people flocking to town for the U.S. Open golf championship. The children, who were raising money to help kids with cancer, were shut down for not having a permit. Even worse, the families were fined a staggering $500! "The message to kids," one of the moms said, "is that there's no American dream."[3]

These stories represent just a fraction of the many cases where aspiring young business owners faced a harsh reality of regulations, permits, and prohibitions. All they wanted to do was sell a drink to a consenting customer. Why all the bureaucracy?

Most parents, if their children experienced a similar encounter with the government, would tell their children to "obey the law." Jump through the legal hoops required, and if they can't—or won't—then shut the business down. This is the conventional wisdom—the path of least resistance.

But what if it's wrong?

What if there is no valid reason why a child should have to seek a permission slip before selling lemonade? What if that child has the *right* to do so?

What if a child really needed to earn some money and decided to break the law and sell lemonade anyway?

What if adults should be able to do the same?

The answers to these questions apply to much more than mere lemonade. These questions, and many more like them, form the foundation of this book—a review of what's right, what's wrong, and in which cases you are justified in saying no when the government tells you to do something you think you shouldn't have to do.

Shall we begin?

NOTES

1. Mark Carlson, "Coralville Police Shut Down Lemonade Stands During RAGBRAI," *Cedar Rapids (IA) Gazette*, August 2, 2011, http://www.thegazette. com/2011/08/02/coralville-police-shut-down-lemon-ade-stands-during-ragbrai.
2. "3 Girls Busted for Illegal Lemonade Stand," NBC News, July 15, 2011, http://www.nbcnews. com/id/43769978/ns/us_news-weird_news/t/girls-busted-illegal-lemonade-stand/.
3. Harry Bradford, "Children's Families Fined $500 for Operating Illegal Lemonade Stand," Huffington Post, June 17, 2011, http://www.huffingtonpost. com/2011/06/17/us-open-lemonade-fine-neighbors-parking_n_878949.html. Following a backlash in the media, the fine was waved and the children were allowed to re-open their stand elsewhere.

"No society can exist unless the laws are respected to a certain degree. The safest way to make laws respected is to make them respectable. When law and morality contradict each other, the citizen has the cruel alternative of either losing his moral sense or losing his respect for the law. These two evils are of equal consequence, and it would be difficult for a person to choose between them."[1]

Frédéric Bastiat

THE RULE OF LAW

Imagine I suddenly stopped you on the street and asked you, "What is a law?" How would you answer? Perhaps you would reply that a law is something the government says you have to do. "Does it matter what type of government?" I might ask. "Are the laws in communist countries or theocratic dictatorships just as valid and binding upon you as those in a democracy or republic?" Now you're probably having to think a little deeper... and maybe you're wishing I had stopped the guy walking behind you instead.

You cautiously answer that a dictator can't just make up the law. The law is something a bit more fundamental—more principled. That's it! You confidently tell me that laws have to be based on a principle.

Not just any principle, you concede, since people can adhere to principles that are simply wrong. It has to be a true principle—a correct one, you add. But now I've backed you into a bit of a corner. "So, everything a government tells a person to do that *isn't* based on a true principle isn't actually a law? Then what do we call that, if not a law?"

Gulp.

Don't worry—most people would struggle to answer these questions. First, they've never really thought about these issues before. Second, they lack the education necessary to answer them adequately. That's not their fault. Government schools—and most private and home schools, for that matter—simply don't teach this stuff.

It's easy to say that "the law" is whatever the government says, but the answer is a bit more complex. Our society uses the word *law* quite liberally, so in a way, yes, a law is a synonym for a mandate from the government. For example, a reporter might point out, "It's against the law in North Korea to criticize the government."[2] Or an environmental activist might say, "The law in many states says that you are not allowed to collect the rain that falls on your property."[3] In the United States of America, one might say that children operating lemonade stands is, in most cities, "breaking the law" if they don't have the necessary paperwork. You get the idea.

Long before you or I were born, a man named Frédéric Bastiat wrote *The Law*, an essay in which he attempted to provide the answers to these questions. Here's how he answered them, and don't worry if it's tricky to follow—we'll analyze what it means in a moment:

Frédéric Bastiat

> What, then, is law? It is the collective organization of the individual right to lawful defense. Each of us has a natural right... to defend his person, his liberty, and his property. These are the three basic requirements of life, and the preservation of any one of them is completely dependent upon the preservation of the other two. For what are our faculties but the extension of our individuality? And what is property but an extension of our faculties?

> If every person has the right to defend—even by force—his person, his liberty, and his property, then it follows that a group of men have the right to organize and support a common force to protect these rights constantly. Thus the principle of collective right—its reason for existing, its lawfulness—is based on individual right. And the

common force that protects this collective right cannot logically have any other purpose or any other mission than that for which it acts as a substitute. Thus, since an individual cannot lawfully use force against the person, liberty, or property of another individual, then the common force—for the same reason—cannot lawfully be used to destroy the person, liberty, or property of individuals or groups.[4]

Okay, let's unpack what he's saying. You and I have the right to defend ourselves and our property, which is an extension of ourselves—the labor we used in the past in exchange for obtaining that property. If somebody wants to harm you, steal your computer, or kidnap you, you are completely justified in fighting back. You have that right—an *individual* right. And nobody gave it to you—it's *natural*. You have it simply because you are a living person.

Let's pretend we've crashed on a remote island inhabited by some native people. Each person in our group has this right of self-defense, so if any of the locals try to harm one of us, we are justified in trying to stop the attack. Suppose we decide to organize a system where one person keeps watch while the others build a shelter or sleep. If a native warrior jumps out of the bushes to hurt you while I'm on watch duty, I can rush to your aid and fight him off on your behalf.

Why is that? I wasn't being attacked, so I wasn't defending myself. Am I doing something wrong because I'm not using my individual right of self-defense? The answer is contained in Bastiat's quote above: we organized to "support a common force to protect [our] rights." We basically formed a government. Every single person has the right to self-defense, and so we all delegated that right to whoever was "in charge" for that shift. It became a *collective* right—something that cannot exist unless each individual in the "collective" has the right that has been delegated.

A "collective" can't come up with rights out of nowhere; the powers of our new government cannot exceed the powers of those who created the government. In other words, the *creature* can't exceed the *creators*. If you decide to make milk from fallen coconuts in an attempt to barter with the locals for other supplies, the island government can't prohibit you from doing so unless you first obtain its permission. It's as Bastiat explained: just as a person is wrong to use force against you—he doesn't have that right—then the "collective" cannot do it for him. We can't delegate a right we do not have to the government.

This, in a nutshell, is *law*—the real kind, based on a true principle and on individual rights. It's what we'll be exploring throughout this book, because understanding what laws a person can justifiably *break* requires know-ing what laws we must *follow*—and why. To break it down further, let's explore some different types of law to see how they relate to what we've learned here.

NATURAL LAW

I can imagine few things more exhilarating than skydiving. If you haven't experienced it, just try to think of the adrenaline that would surge through your body as you fall from a high altitude to the earth below. As you train to learn the ins and outs of jumping out of an airplane, your instructor would explain the care and attention that goes into packing your parachute. Your life, quite literally, depends upon that neatly folded piece of thin fabric.

The reason why, of course, is obvious. If you find yourself plummeting towards a very hard surface be-low and something goes wrong when you try to deploy your parachute, you're likely going to end up as a big mess on somebody's property.

Gravity is unforgiving and always present. Drop something that is heavier than air and it will fall. This re-action is so predictable and observable that we don't just call it by its name. Instead, we call it the *law* of gravity.

Forgive me for pointing out something that is al-ready painfully evident to you: gravity does not exist because a bunch of politicians got together and decided to pass a law requiring objects to fall to the earth. A majority vote did not create this condition, nor can a vote stop it from happening. It exists, rather, because it is a law of nature—a governing rule that is self-evident.

Self-evident. Does that ring a bell? Thomas Jefferson used the term in the Declaration of Independence when he talked about fundamental truths that were among the reasons the American colonists seceded from Britain in order to govern themselves. As you may recall, here's what he wrote:

> We hold these truths to be self-evident, that all men are created equal, that they are endowed by their Creator with certain unalienable rights, that among these are life, liberty, and the pursuit of happiness.

What Jefferson is referring to are natural laws, or self-evident truths, that are observable and indisputable statements that clearly reflect man's relationship one to another. When we are born we are all equal, no matter our parents' race, religion, location, or lineage. And, importantly, we all have the right to our life, our liberty, and our future self-determination.

Few today understand this, but in America's first few decades it was widely understood. (Except for that part about race, sadly.) John Quincy Adams—the sixth U.S. president and son of John Adams—once noted that the colonists had "renounc[ed]... all claims to chartered rights as Englishmen. Henceforth their charter was the Declaration of Independence. Their rights, the natural rights of mankind."[5] Natural rights. Natural law. Their rights didn't come from the English government, nor from a document or majority vote. They were appealing to a higher, more fundamental law.

Some might think that Jefferson coined the term or sparked a more widespread understanding of natural law, but that's not really the case. Jefferson himself said, some fifty years after he helped draft the Declaration of Independence, that it was merely "intended to be an expression of the American mind"[6] at the time it was written. People already understood the priority of natural law over the "laws" that a government might make. If you look at what colonial legislatures were saying before the Declaration was written in 1776, you'll find similar language showing their agreement.

As just one example, consider the Resolutions of the House of Representatives of Massachusetts, written on October 29, 1765. This document served as a defiant objection to the infamous Stamp Act—an egregious new tax on every piece of printed paper the colonists used. Notice the references to natural, self-evident rights contained in just the first two of fourteen total resolutions:

> 1. Resolved, that there are certain *essential Rights* of the British Constitution of government which are founded in the *Law of God and Nature*, and are *common Rights* of Mankind.

> 2. Resolved, that the inhabitants of this Province are *unalienably entitled* to those *essential rights in common with all men*: and that *no law of society can, consistent with the law of God and nature, divest them of those rights.*[7]

John Locke

Ever heard of John Locke? He was a philosopher who deserves much of the credit for getting so many Americans to understand these ideas. Indeed, many of the Founding Fathers—especially Jefferson—were strongly influenced by Locke's writings. Nearly a century before the American Revolution, Locke published his *Second Treatise on Government*, a book in which he explained what natural law is. Let's consider one of his arguments a step at a time:

To properly understand political power and trace its origins, we must consider the state that all people are in naturally. That is a state of perfect freedom of acting and disposing of their own possessions and persons as they think fit within the bounds of the law of nature.[8]

Locke is asking us to imagine a situation in which you and I might interact with one another in an environment where there is no government, just like the island example we discussed earlier. This is our "natural state" of "perfect freedom" because there are no *artificial* (man-made) restraints on our actions. Instead, we are only bound by laws that are *natural*—the literal opposite of artificial. Locke continues:

People in this state do not have to ask permission to act or depend on the will of others to arrange matters on their behalf. The natural state is also one of equality in which all power and jurisdiction is reciprocal and no one has more than another.[9]

This idea surely sounds intoxicating. No permission needed for anything? Finally, freedom! But focus on what Locke is saying in the second half of that statement. Our freedom—our "natural state"—is equal to that of others. We don't have the power to control others, just as others don't have any power to control us. There are no kings or presidents in nature. Power is also reciprocal, Locke says, meaning that if you punch somebody, they're justified in punching you back. If you steal from a neighbor, they're justified in using the same power against you.

This concept of equality was important to Locke, just as it later was to the American rebels. Recall that Jefferson's first self-evident truth—the one he listed at the top because it was so important—was that "*all men* are created equal." Given its importance, Locke explained it a little more:

> It is evident that all human beings—as creatures belonging to the same species and rank and born indiscriminately with all the same natural advantages and faculties—are equal amongst themselves.[10]

So in a state of nature, we're all equal; gravity, of course, applies to everybody. The laws that govern our interactions with one another must, therefore, be consistent, without exception. We all, for example, have the right to life. So one way to figure out if a law is *natural* is whether it applies to everybody equally. Welfare programs that force some people to pay for things to benefit other people don't qualify, nor does a wartime draft that makes only men of a certain age fight in the military. But a law against murder does qualify—it applies to every single person. Murder is wrong, whether or not a government says so.

Even though Locke explained natural law in a compelling way that influenced America's founders, he didn't pioneer the idea. Various philosophers had been discussing these things for centuries—guys like Hugo Grotius of Holland (1583-1645), Thomas Hobbes of England (1588-1679), Francisco Suárez of Spain (1548-1617), and especially Thomas Aquinas of Italy (1225-1274). The concept goes back as far as Cicero (106-43 BC) and Aristotle (384-322 BC). Generally, these people—and many others—taught that certain universal, moral laws exist that are observable in nature, just like gravity.

Hobbes described natural law as "a precept, or general rule, found out by reason."[11] Grotius wrote that it "proceeds from the essential traits implanted in man."[12] Cicero discussed natural, or "true" law in detail:

> True law is right reason in agreement with nature; it is of universal application, unchanging and everlasting; it summons to duty by its commands, and averts from wrongdoing by its prohibitions...
>
> It is a sin to try to alter this law, nor is it allowable to repeal any part of it, and it is impossible to abolish entirely. We cannot be freed from its

obligations by senate or people, and we need not look outside ourselves for an expounder or interpreter of it. And there will not be different laws at Rome and Athens, or different laws now and in the future, but one eternal and unchangeable law will be valid for all nations and all times...[13]

Locke's more detailed explanation merely summarized what philosophers had long been observing: man-made law is subject to a higher law. It's no surprise, then, that the framers of the U.S. Constitution used the same format in what's called the Supremacy Clause, which says that the Constitution overrides any state law that conflicts with it. For example, the Constitution says that states must have a republican form of government. If a bunch of communists hatched a coordinated campaign to move to New Jersey, gain the majority of elected positions in the state legislature, and then vote to govern New Jersey under a Communist dictatorship, would that be valid? Not according to the Constitution. It, as the higher law, would override this communist plot; the attempted takeover would be unconstitutional, and thus illegal.

Natural law works similarly. Because it is the higher law—it came first, before any government's laws did—anything contrary to it is invalid and void. If Congress passed a law outlawing gravity, it would be of no effect. And if a legislature passed a law saying murder was okay, that would also be invalid; murder is always wrong, even if somebody casts a vote to legalize it. As the famous English judge William Blackstone once wrote, "No human laws are of any validity, if contrary to [natural law]; and such of them as are valid, derive all their authority... from this original."[14] Man-made laws have to be in harmony with natural law to be valid.

And who casts these votes, anyway? We sometimes call them "lawmakers," which is an absurd title. It reminds me of so-called "rainmakers"—people who believe that their ceremonial rituals can cause rain to fall. These people don't *make* rain. Similarly, politicians don't *make* law. At best, they can merely articulate a natural law more precisely to apply it to our modern lives, applying existing law to the age in which we live.

For example, natural law states that you cannot steal from another person; this is an observably harmful action against an innocent individual. So a politician could propose a law based on this natural law, which lists specific types of theft and punishments for each. Employees should not embezzle money from their employers; children should not steal from a store; hackers should not leak private information belonging to another person. These would be valid laws, as they are tied to a natural law. Even then, the politician is not so much a "lawmaker" as he is a "law explainer."

Lysander Spooner, a nineteenth-century political philosopher, emphasized this point further, noting that a politician's departure from natural law leads to a situation in which their mandates lose authority and, therefore, do not deserve our allegiance:

Lysander Spooner

> Lawmakers, as they call themselves, can add nothing to [the supreme law], nor take anything from it. Therefore all their laws, as they call them—that is, all the laws of their own making—have no color of authority or obligation. It is a falsehood to call them laws; for there is nothing in them that either creates men's duties or rights, or enlightens them as to their duties or rights. There is consequently nothing binding or obligatory about them. And nobody is bound to take the least notice of them, unless it be to trample them under foot, as usurpations.[15]

Here we're beginning to see an argument to justify breaking a law if it violates natural law; we'll dig into this deeper in the next chapter. For now, let's summarize this section. Natural law deals with observable principles found in nature that come before, and thus supersede, the government. To qualify, a law must apply equally to every person—just like gravity. And natural laws don't change over time; it's always wrong, for example, to steal something from another person. Finally, a government's mandate can only be legitimate if it's based upon a natural law. If a mandate conflicts with natural law, then it's invalid.

Now that we've established what a *natural* law looks like, we have to explain its opposite—the *arbitrary* type that isn't observable, pre-existing, or equally binding. Sadly, as you'll soon realize, this describes a large portion of the laws that governments enforce today.

POSITIVE LAW

"Humans evolved from primordial chemicals reacting to energy."

Perhaps you consider this a controversial claim, and you might reject its truthfulness. But many people believe this reflects reality, including teachers who stand in front of students all over the world teaching it as a legitimate and likely theory. Some believe so strongly in this theory of evolution that they claim it is fact. These people are actually *assuming* that it is fact, even though they are basing their views on theories derived from an incomplete fossil record rather than absolute knowledge. What they are doing is "positing" an argument, as in "I posit that humans evolved from primordial soup."

The term *posit* is derived from the Latin *positus*, as is the related word *positive*. We sometimes use this word to convey affirmation or approval, as in "Think positive thoughts!" In other cases, the word is used as an assumption, as in "I'm positive I've heard that song before." When describing the opposite of natural law, we use the term *positive law* in the context of "assumption." Just like claiming the theory of evolution is fact, positive law is also a dogmatic decree—a collection of mandates where "lawmakers" assume that their theories and ideas are factual and real. Noah Webster's 1828 dictionary makes this clear—one of the several definitions he offered of the term *positive* is "settled by arbitrary appointment; opposed to natural."[16]

We used the example of gravity to explain how natural law is observable, pre-existing, and equally binding upon everybody. Positive law is the opposite of each of these criterion. If you and some friends create a new card game and establish some rules to govern how participants must play, your neighbor can't comprehend the rules merely by observing the cards. The rules were made *after* the game was created, not before. And those rules are only binding on those who play—a woman living in Singapore, for example, is obviously not bound by what's happening in the game.

Since we're talking about government—an organization of people in a certain geographic area—a better example would be of you and some friends forming an exclusive club. Your new organization would likely have rules to admit new members and expel members for violating your code of conduct. Like the card game, these club rules would not be observable by outsiders—you'd have to explain them to those who want to join. Your club's rules don't pre-date the club itself. And if one of your club's rules is that everybody should wear striped clothing on Saturdays, you can't compel your non-member siblings and friends to dress accordingly.

These may be silly examples, but they help illustrate the arbitrariness of positive (arbitrary) law—a set of rules that, by default, oppose natural law. You'll recall that natural law is tied to natural rights—for example, the right to life, liberty, and the pursuit of happiness. Positive law, on the other hand, involves the creation of "rights" that wouldn't exist without the government granting them to you. The Declaration of Independence recognizes the natural rights of life and liberty, whereas the 1936 Constitution of the Union of Soviet Socialist Republics (USSR) establishes various *positive* rights that did not exist until the government created (and enforced) them. Under a list in section 10, titled "Fundamental Rights and Duties of Citizens," we find the following:

- The right to employment
- The right to rest and leisure
- The right to maintenance (being taken care of) in old age and also in case of sickness or loss of capacity to work
- The right to education

These are all important things, of course—but as positive rights they become problematic. To understand why, we first have to understand the relationship between rights and duties. In natural law, your only duty is to *not* do things to others that violate their rights. For this reason, natural rights are sometimes referred to as "negative rights," because the action required of other people is negative, or *not doing something*. Your right to life carries a negative duty on others to *not* kill you. Your right to liberty means that other people *can't* lock you up in their basement. Negative rights carry negative duties—basically, don't do bad things to other people.

You can see where this is going, right? Just as negative rights lead to negative duties, positive rights create positive duties. And rather than *not* doing something to others, positive duties mean that you *must* do certain things for other people. A positive right to "employment," as was the case in the USSR, means that business owners had to provide jobs to certain people, even if it was against their wishes. A positive right of old people to be cared for means that younger people must be forced to pay for that maintenance. Saying people have the right to education means that everybody has to pay money to hire teachers to make it happen. Positive rights create obligations on people to do certain things—things they wouldn't have to do under natural law or in the absence of a government making up those laws.

Jack Phillips is the owner of Masterpiece Cakeshop in Lakewood, Colorado. He's a Christian that strives to live his faith both personally and professionally. For example, he has refused to create cakes that celebrate Halloween or carry profane or anti-family messages. His decision to operate his own business consistent with his religious beliefs became the subject of national controversy when Charles Craig and David Mullins walked into his shop one day in 2012, requesting a cake be made for their wedding reception.

Jack politely declined. "Sorry guys, I don't make cakes for same-sex weddings," he told the couple.[17] Denied their cake, David and Charles filed a complaint with the state civil rights commission; Colorado law prohibits business owners from denying service to customers based on their sexual orientation. The commission unsurprisingly ruled against the cake maker, and their decision was upheld in court. "As a creative professional and a businessman," Jack said, "I shouldn't have to give up my freedom—my religion—when I open a bakery."[18]

But the law had created a positive right—for homosexual individuals to receive service from all businesses—and therefore had to impose a duty upon all business owners.

John Austin

Positive law has been around as long as governments have; no known government has confined itself entirely to natural law. As long as governments have been bossing people around, those in power have been coming up with arguments to try to justify their mandates as legitimate and deserving of our obedience. In modern times, one of positive law's biggest cheerleaders was John Austin, a British legal theorist whose writings strongly impacted the English government in the nineteenth century. Austin argued that laws are not merely governing principles related to natural rights, but "imperium oriented" dictates from authorized sources. (*Imperium* should conjure up images of the empire in *Star Wars*, as that's what the word means—a government with absolute power.) In other words, whatever those in authority wanted to make happen was suddenly as valid a law as any natural law.

"The existence of law is one thing," Austin wrote. "Its merit or demerit is another."[19] He tried to argue, basically, that we could disagree with a ruler's command all we wanted, but since the ruler had issued the command, it becomes *automatically authoritative* by virtue of the power used to create it. Where natural law requires the chaining of any "lawmaking" to an underlying, pre-existing law that applies to everybody, Austin and those who agree with him believe that *there shouldn't be any chains*. Whatever the government says, goes. The people in charge are all the authority that's needed.

In contrast, natural law's authority is either God, for those who are religious, or the sovereignty of the individual who possesses natural rights. Positive law's only claim to authority is the ability to impose that authority by force. Imagine a gangster ordering people around in a neighborhood he "controls." What does the gangster do to ensure compliance? He doesn't point to a signed contract. He doesn't ask nicely. He doesn't negotiate. No, the gangster would tap his gun and point it at the defiant person as a way to coerce compliance. This is the "authority" of positive law—the authority's willingness to hurt those who fail to obey their arbitrary commands. Sadly, the gang analogy is not an unfounded one when it comes to today's governments. It's no wonder philosopher and author Ayn Rand referred to a government based on positive law as "a mob held together by institutionalized gang-rule."[20]

Think for a moment what a government might look like that confined itself to only enforcing natural laws. It would probably be pretty small, right? You'd basically just need a police force to help defend people from bad guys. But positive law leads to governments that legislate on all sorts of things: how long one must attend school to cut another person's hair, what people are allowed to put in their bodies, who can open a business, what people can do with their property, and on and on. The government would have to be large, not just to debate the many complexities of these "laws"— how and when they apply, and to whom—but also to enforce them.

Most people are unaware of just how big governments grow in a positive law system. You likely know about federal, state, county, and city governments—each of which pass a voluminous number of laws—but there are more. Depending on where you live, you might also be governed by a water conservancy district, mosquito abatement district, recreation authority, cemetery district, or a drainage district. The growth of government is a symptom of positive law, and demonstrates the wisdom of Thomas Jefferson's observation: "The natural progress of things is for liberty to yield, and government to gain ground."[21]

One consequence of bossing people around in so many aspects of their lives and making them do things they don't feel are necessary is that they might have an increased desire to break the law since the rules are so arbitrary. If you're playing a game and somebody is constantly changing the many confusing rules, chances are you'll get frustrated and consider cheating. This reaction is an important one to analyze, which we'll do in the next chapter.

For now, let's review: Natural laws are observable, pre-existing, and equally binding. They protect natural rights, which we possess without any government saying so. And they create negative duties—a requirement only that other people not do things that would violate those rights. Positive laws, on the other hand, are not readily observable, only exist because somebody made them up, and are only binding on those under the supposed authority of the government that enforces them. They create positive rights, which only exist because the government said so. And those create positive duties, forcing people to do things they otherwise wouldn't have to do.

It's one thing to determine the source of a law's authority and to whom it applies. But who gets to decide what those laws are? Today's governments mostly rely upon legislatures to create, debate, and vote on new laws. Before we discuss the problems with this approach, let's take a look at another method—one that involves judges determining what the law is.

COMMON LAW

When you think of England, a king or queen comes to mind, right? But the country's political makeup has undergone a lot of changes from centuries past due to warring kingdoms constantly seeking power over one another. For example, in the year 1066 A.D. when Norman soldiers invaded the island, England was comprised of approximately eight large kingdoms, which were themselves collections of "hundred groups"—privately owned and independently governed landholdings.

Can you imagine trying to control so many different groups of people? The Normans organized counties to administer local laws and established local courts to settle disputes that arose in each community. In the decades that followed, different court systems and judges resolved issues that were brought to them, especially as it pertained to land—who owned what, and where, and under what circumstances.

As later judges and Englishmen were working through disputes, they would turn to the decisions of the past as a guide for what they should do. This is what is called *common law*—a set of rules governing how people should act, based on the judicial observations and decisions that shaped society in previous years. These decisions were also influenced both by rulings from the king and his court and by local customs.

Some people confuse common law with natural law, but they are distinct. First off, common law only applied to a specific group of people, rather than all people everywhere. As common law was a creation of these particular circumstances in England, it essentially has applied only to countries that were colonized at some point in time by England (or Great Britain, or the United Kingdom). Examples include Wales, Northern

Ireland, the United States, Canada, Australia, Kenya, New Zealand, South Africa, India, and many more. If you find yourself in China, you won't be the beneficiary of common law.

While natural law relies upon observable truths that apply equally to everybody, common law relies on decisions made by a few people in the past. Those outcomes were often favorable towards property rights and individual liberty, but this was not always the case. Many mistakes and bad rulings have been made in the past; common law effectively requires binding yourself to previous decisions, whether they were good or not, merely because these similar disputes were already settled. It's basically a government of tradition.

Now, one reason why there is confusion between common and natural law is because judges under the common law weren't considered to be "making" law or "legislating from the bench," as you'll sometimes hear in today's criticisms of the courts. These judges were tasked with looking to the past for guidance, and to the community for moral direction. They aimed not to create law, but to *find* it.

The printing press helped with this endeavor. As written records were made of the court decisions, it became easier for judges to understand what others had decided in cases that related to the ones they were dealing with. These judicial precedents were considered to have the force of law—not merely because a past judge had made a decision, but because of the principle that similar cases should be similarly decided. Conformity was key.

When the right to a jury was enshrined in the Magna Carta in 1215—after some rebellious barons demanded a recognition of certain rights from the unpopular king—those serving on juries decided cases under the common law, based in part on local custom. Therein lies common law's weakness.

Think for a moment: what if a community's custom was to rob food from people named Joshua on Mondays? Or to stone redheads in the town square during a full moon? These odd cultural practices would be wrong according to our understanding of natural law, and yet according to common law, juries would declare those who participated in them to be innocent because it was acceptable according to their customs. But is that a good idea? Should customs have the force of law? Is it okay to do something merely because that thing has been done by others in the past?

One appealing aspect of this system of law is the fact that it is decentralized, meaning that government enforcement is localized and dispersed, rather than concentrated at one level and forced upon everybody. If a dictator makes a decree, that becomes binding upon each person who lives on land the dictator claims to control. But when a judge "found" the law in a particular case, it primarily affected the individuals whose case was being considered in court.

And therein lies another interesting aspect of common law: the judge could only make a decision when he was asked to do so. He wasn't a dictator, and there was no activism—if there were no disputes to resolve, then the judge had no business to attend to. Think of it like today's firefighters—unlike the police, who proactively roam about the city in search of people doing things that are illegal, firefighters only affect your life if you find yourself in need of their services.

One of the most important aspects of common law was the stability and certainty it provided. Like the path of a river that has been carved into the earth over time through many water droplets passing by, the body of law established through many court decisions striving for uniformity would be difficult to quickly alter to any degree. It takes a long time for just rules to be discovered and consistently applied in a common law system enough to be lawfully binding upon any case with similar circumstances.

Why is that important? Well, imagine you're a traveling salesman in seventeenth-century England. If each community has different laws about where you can travel, who you can speak to, or what times of day you can approach people in the town square, it will be difficult for you to be successful—especially if those rules can be changed by a simple vote at a town council. You may get out of the business completely, worried that the arbitrary and changing nature of the law makes it difficult to plan a business when you don't know what tomorrow will bring.

Instead, under a common law system—where the laws are a byproduct of decades or centuries of decisions—you have a more predictable environment in which to build your business. Perhaps throughout England, judges had long decided that you could freely travel in public areas, speak to anyone you wish as long as you weren't trespassing, and approach anyone in the town square during daylight hours. Knowing of these time-tested decisions and the consistency with which judges ruled on cases that dealt with these issues, you would be able to move forward with certainty, not worried about the rules suddenly changing on you.

As you'll see in the next section, these are advantages over what we have in today's legal systems, where top-down, centralized government systems constantly change the "law" and directly interfere in the lives of their citizens.

STATUTORY LAW

Gideon Tucker was a judge in New York during the mid-nineteenth century. In 1866, he presided over a case dealing with the estate of a man who had died. The man's widow had been given bad advice by her attorney about his property. The problem, said the judge, "arose from want of diligent watchfulness in respect to legislative changes." In other words, the widow and her attorney were unaware of how elected officials had changed the laws dealing with estate planning and inheritance—laws that affected her case and the distribution of her late husband's property.

Gideon Tucker

Being aware of many other instances in which legislators had changed things in ways that negatively affected the people they supposedly represent, Tucker observed: "No man's life, liberty, or property are safe while the legislature is in session."[22]

This ever-present threat to life, liberty, and property is the result of a system of *statutory law*—when the "law" is nothing more than whatever those in charge of the government say it is. These mandates are written down as "statutes," or rules of conduct.

Perhaps you already see the problem here. Whereas natural law is unchanging, as it is based on universal truths, and common law is very slow to change, since it relies upon long-held traditions and previously made decisions, statutory law has no such anchor. There is no foundation; it can change over and over and over again. A legislature could pass a law requiring adult drivers to wear seat belts, repeal that law the following year, and then re-enact it the year after that.

This constant flux in the law led James Madison to express some concern about it. In *Federalist* No. 62, he wrote:

> It will be of little avail to the people, that the laws are made by men of their own choice, if the laws be so voluminous that they cannot be read, or so incoherent that they cannot be understood; if they be repealed or revised before they are promulgated, or undergo such incessant changes that no man, who knows what the law is today, can guess what it will be tomorrow. Law is defined to be a rule of action; but how

James Madison

can that be a rule, which is little known, and less fixed?[23]

Read that again if it sounded confusing—it's powerful. At the dawn of American self-government, Madison was basically saying that it would be pointless if the "law" was a mess—long, complex, constantly changing. For example, who would think that something simple like selling lemonade requires permits, regulatory compliance, and paying a fee? We cannot have confidence in a system that undergoes "such incessant changes that no man, who knows what the law is today, can guess what it will be tomorrow." Remember our example of the salesman in a common law system? Predictability allows him to proceed with his business and get on with life. But a statutory system creates constant uncertainty. Like Judge Tucker said, we are threatened every time elected officials are voting. Nobody knows what will happen, and everything is up in the air. Anything is possible, as long as there are enough votes—even making it a crime to own a feather.

That's the situation Pastor Robert Soto found himself in during a religious ceremony in 2006. Agents from the U.S. Department of Interior infiltrated the ceremonial circle of the Lipan Apache tribe members meeting at a community center in Texas. Soto's crime?

Robert Soto

He was in possession of prohibited feathers. Bald eagles and golden eagles are protected by the Migratory Bird Treaty Act and the Eagle Protection Act. Possession of their feathers by unapproved persons can lead to 15 years in federal prison and a $250,000 fine.

Many native tribes use these feathers in their religious practices, as the eagle is considered sacred. And other tribes have approval to use them because they are a federally recognized tribe. Unfortunately for Soto, the Lipan Apaches aren't recognized, and are therefore prohibited from using the feathers. This is especially silly given that the tribe has been around for more than three centuries—longer than Texas has been a part of the United States of America. Soto's group is recognized by that state, Spain, and Mexico—but not the federal government, despite petitions asking for the recognition to be made. Their petitions have been denied.[24]

What was most surprising for Soto was the intrusion into a religious ceremony and setting. Federal agents claimed that because the group had advertised the ceremony in the newspaper, and because money was exchanged at the event, it was not sacred. The government had, in Soto's mind, "established what I like to call 'unknown laws,'" allowing them to conveniently "nullify the sacredness of a gathering."[25]

Can you see the problem with this legal approach? One day you could be declared a criminal, not because you knew of a longstanding law that you intentionally violated, but because your action was deemed by politicians to be punishable. Or perhaps, like Soto, you might find yourself targeted by government employees who creatively interpret ever-changing rules in their favor. In response to this, you might protest, "I can't be guilty if I don't know about the law I broke!"

You'd be wrong.

There's a long-established legal principle that *ignorantia juris non excusat*, Latin for "ignorance of the law is no excuse." Steve Martin once performed a comedy sketch where he suggested telling a judge "I forgot" in response to any criminal prosecution. Caught stealing from another person at gunpoint? Just tell the judge "I forgot armed robbery was illegal," Martin joked.[26]

Of course, this is humorous because everybody knows that pointing a gun at somebody or stealing from them is wrong. Nobody can claim that they forgot or weren't aware that that was against the law because these are examples of natural laws. But in a system of statutory law, how can we keep track of every law that is changed and make sure we are in compliance?

We can't. At the level of the federal government alone, Congress has been adding an average of 55 new crimes each year.[27] There are now around 5,000 federal crimes you can be punished for, and that doesn't include all the regulations that have criminal penalties, nor all the crimes created at the state and local levels of government.[28] Here are just a few examples of federal crimes:

- Letting your snowmobile idle for more than 3 minutes in Yellowstone National Park.[29]
- Selling self-pressurized animal food without warning people to not spray it in their eyes.[30]
- Pruning coffee trees during the elfin-woods warbler's peak breeding season.[31]
- Selling "spaghetti sauce with meat" if it's less than 6% meat.[32]
- Chasing away a polar bear with your truck.[33]
- Importing moist bamboo into the United States.[34]
- Selling a baby pacifier with leather or chain attached to it.[35]
- Bringing your dog to the post office if it's not a service dog or there on official business.[36]

Girod's herbal products

Sometimes federal statutes are based on natural law—for example, establishing a criminal penalty for murder, theft, or kidnapping—but they are more often based on positive laws, like those listed above. Actions that don't harm another person are punished merely because a group of politicians or bureaucrats decided that they wanted to punish that type of activity.

If this seems rather odd to you, imagine being Samuel Girod. He's an Amish farmer and a convicted criminal, sentenced to six years in prison in 2017.[37] No, he didn't kill somebody. There was no assault. Nobody had their property stolen. His crime? He had improperly labeled some health products he sold, processed them in a facility that wasn't registered with the U.S. Food and Drug Administration, and fought the investigation that followed.[38]

There was no victim of these supposed crimes. The prosecutor could not produce a single witness claiming to have been harmed by Girod in any way. The government had simply decided that what he had done was wrong and punished him for not jumping through arbitrarily established regulatory hoops.

"I do not consent," Girod told the judge, arguing that the court didn't have jurisdiction over him—a concept we'll explore later in the book. Outside the courthouse, supporters gathered in anticipation of the verdict. T.J. Roberts, a college student at a nearby university, held a sign that said, "I don't need the FDA to protect me from an Amish farmer." He commented to a reporter:

> I feel what happened here is an example of judges making the law. What the FDA did here is an example of executive overreach in which they are choosing what Americans can put in or on their own bodies. I struggle to find where the victim is in this and where the crime was committed.[39]

Statutory law allows for—and even invites—such arbitrary crimes, punishing innocent people who have harmed nobody. No underlying morality is needed to decide what is right and wrong. All that's needed is a majority vote or a simple decree from a king, president, or other executive. And as we've seen, it doesn't really matter whether the "criminal" knew about the law before breaking it. This didn't matter as much centuries ago, but it does matter today, as one legal commentator pointed out:

> The rule that "ignorance of the law is no excuse" was born at a time when there were fewer than a dozen common law felonies, and all those crimes stemmed from and mirrored a commonly shared moral code. Today, the criminal law is a collection of social preferences. Some of them are obvious and reflect common sense notions of wrongfulness, but many reflect only a legislative judgment. It may indeed be a bad idea to ride a manatee for fun, but it is unlikely that anyone would know it was a federal crime—until they read this paper or were prosecuted for it.[40]

Judge Tucker was right. Our life, liberty, and property are not safe when legislatures are in session—or when bureaucrats are working every day—because at any moment, in a system of statutory law, we might find ourselves doing something illegal without even knowing it.

Children selling lemonade throughout the "land of the free" have no idea that they could be shut down or fined—or even jailed if they resist. They are innocently unaware that statutes compel them to obtain permission slips before offering their delicious drinks to consenting customers.

The question we need to explore is: despite engaging in illegal conduct, are they in the wrong?

NOTES

1. Frédéric Bastiat, *The Law* (Salt Lake City: Libertas Institute, 2013), 7-8.
2. Andrew Salmon, "What North Koreans Really Think of Kim Jong-un," *Telegraph*, April 8, 2012, http://www.telegraph.co.uk/news/worldnews/asia/north-korea/9191998/What-North-Koreans-really-think-of-Kim-Jong-un.html.
3. Jeff Guo, "It Is Actually Illegal in Colorado to Collect the Rain That Falls on Your Home," *Washington Post*, March 24, 2015, https://www.washingtonpost.com/blogs/govbeat/wp/2015/03/24/it-is-actually-illegal-in-colorado-to-collect-the-rain-that-falls-on-your-home/.
4. Bastiat, *The Law*, 2.
5. John Quincy Adams, *The Jubilee of the Constitution* (New York: Bedford, 1839), 9.
6. Paul Leicester Ford, ed., *The Works of Thomas Jefferson*, vol. 12 (New York: G. P. Putnam's Sons, 1905), 409.
7. Quoted in William Knox et al., eds., *The Controversy Between Great Britain and Her Colonies Reviewed* (London: privately printed for J. Almon, 1769) xxxviii-xxxix; emphasis added.
8. John Locke, *Two Treatises on Government: A Translation into Modern English* (Manchester, UK: Industrial Systems Research, 2009), 106.
9. Ibid.
10. Ibid.
11. Thomas Hobbes, *Leviathan* (London: Forgotten Books, 2008), 89.
12. Quoted in Frederick Copleston, ed., *A History of Philosophy*, vol. 3 (New York: Continuum International Publishing Group, 2003), 330.

13. Robert T. Radford, ed., *Cicero: A Study in the True Origins of Republican Philosophy* (New York: Rodopi B. V., 2002), 43.

14. Quoted in Harold C. Syrett, ed., *The Papers of Alexander Hamilton*, vol. 26 (New York: Columbia University Press, 1961), 85.

15. Charles Shively, ed., *The Collected Works of Lysander Spooner* (Weston: M & S Press, 1971), 3.

16. *Webster's Dictionary*, 1829 ed., s.v. "positive," http://webstersdictionary1828.com/Dictionary/positive.

17. Robert Barnes, "The Spurned Gay Couple, the Colorado Baker and the Years Spent Waiting for the Supreme Court," *Denver Post*, August 14, 2017, http://www.denverpost.com/2017/08/14/colorado-gay-wedding-cake-case/.

18. Ibid.

19. John Austin, *Lectures on Jurisprudence, Or, The Philosophy of Positive Law*, ed. Robert Campbell (London: John Murray, 1869), 220.

20. Ayn Rand, *Capitalism: The Unknown Ideal* (New York: Signet, 1967), 379.

21. H.A. Washington, ed., *The works of Thomas Jefferson*, vol. 2 (New York: Townsend Mac Coun., 1884), 404.

22. Gideon John Tucker, *Reports of Cases Argued and Determined in the Surrogate's Court of the County of New York*, vol. 1 (New York: Banks & Brothers, 1870), 249.

23. Alexander Hamilton, James Madison, and John Jay, *The Federalist on The New Constitution, Written in the Year 1788* (Hallowell: Glazier, Masters & Smith, 1842), 287.

24. Abby Phillip, "Why Eagle Feathers Could Land This Native American Pastor in Prison," *Washington Post*, May 27, 2015, https://www.washingtonpost.com/news/acts-of-faith/wp/2015/05/26/why-eagle-feath-ers-could-land-this-native-american-pastor-in-prison/.

25. Daniel A. Flores, "Robert Soto Fought for Years to Have Ceremonial Feathers Returned to Local Lipan Apaches," *The Monitor*, January 29, 2017, http://www.

themonitor.com/life/vidasunday/article_8c064efe-
e4cb-11e6-bfd3-7383bea2ba24.html.

26. "Steve Martin's Monologue," *Saturday Night Live*,
    season 3, episode 9, directed by Dave Wilson and
    James Signorelli, aired January 21, 1978, (New
    York: NBC Studios, 1978), http://snltranscripts.
    jt.org/77/77imono.phtml.

27. John Baker, "Revisiting the Explosive Growth
    of Federal Crimes," Heritage Foundation, June
    16, 2008, http://www.heritage.org/report/
    revisiting-the-explosive-growth-federal-crimes.

28. Joycelyn M. Pollock, *Criminal Law* (New York:
    Routledge, 2016), 49.

29. 18 USC § 1865 & 36 CFR §7.13(l)(13).

30. 21 USC §333 & 21 CFR §501.17(a)(1).

31. 16 USC §1375(b) & 50 CFR §17.41(e)(2)(i).

32. 21 USC §§610, 676 & 9 CFR §319.307.

33. 16 USC §1375 & 50 CFR §18.34(b)(2)(ii).

34. 7 USC §7734(a)(1)(B) & 7 CFR §319.40–5(a).

35. 15 USC §1254, 16 CFR §1500.18(a)(8) & 1511.6.

36. 18 USC §3061 & 39 CFR §232.1(j).

37. Bill Estep, "Amish Man Convicted of Selling Improperly
    Labeled Health Products," *Lexington (KY) Herald
    Leader*, March 2, 2017, http://www.kentucky.com/
    news/state/article135986318.html.

38. Greg Kocher, "Amish Farmer Sold Herbal Health
    Products. He's Going to Prison for 6 Years," *Lexington
    (KY) Herald Leader*, June 30, 2017, http://www.ken-
    tucky.com/news/local/crime/article159031869.html.

39. Ibid.

40. Paul Rosenzweig, "Ignorance of the Law Is No Excuse,
    But It Is Reality," Heritage Foundation, June 17, 2013,
    http://www.heritage.org/crime-and-justice/report/
    ignorance-the-law-no-excuse-it-reality.

"If ... the ability to tell right from wrong should turn out to have anything to do with the ability to think, then we must be able to 'demand' its exercise from every sane person, no matter how erudite or ignorant, intelligent or stupid, he may happen to be."[1]

Hannah Arendt

WHAT IS WRONG?

In November 2014, 90-year-old Arnold Abbott began handing out plates of hot food to homeless people in a south Florida park, as he had done many times before. But this time was different. An approaching policeman grabbed his arm and said, "Drop that plate right now," almost as if Abbott was holding a gun, he later remarked.[2]

He was charged with violating the law for feeding the homeless—a law that the city council had passed just a week prior. That law limited where feeding sites could be located, required that people providing food obtain a permit, and required food providers to also provide portable toilets, hand-washing stations, and ensure that the food is precisely maintained at certain temperatures.

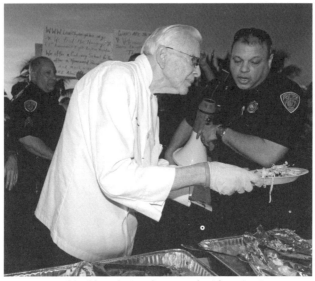

Arnold Abbott being threatened with a citation

Abbott created the Love Thy Neighbor Fund in 1991 as a tribute to his wife who had passed away. The organization continued the important work that they had enjoyed doing together, feeding the homeless and supporting the needy.

Despite being punished by the city for his compassionate act, Abbott continued his work—and continued violating the law. He racked up four additional citations, each of which involved a fine of up to $500 and up to 60 days in jail. Commenting on the controversy, Abbott said:

> The city passed an ordinance requiring us to have a Porta-Potty. It's ridiculous. The whole thing was designed to rid [the city] of its homeless. Police told me anyone who touches a pan... anyone who is involved, will be arrested.[3]

"The reason we're not going to back down," explained a rabbi accomplice who had been helping feed the needy, "is because it's so unjust to put people in jail for helping other people."[4] Abbott wasn't that worried. "I'm not afraid of jail," he said. "I'm not looking to go, but if I have to, I will."[5] Fortunately, he didn't have to. The attention of the world focused briefly on Abbott's case as the international media widely published the story of a simple, old man helping the homeless and being harassed by the government because of it. The city stopped enforcing the law due to negative publicity. Abbott won—at least for a while.

Let's contrast this story against another one. Wilhelm Keitel was born in a small German village in 1882. As the oldest son, he hoped to one day take over management of Helmscherode, the 600-acre estate his grandfather had purchased years before. His family had been involved in land ownership and management for generations; he had farmer's blood in his veins. But his father refused to relinquish control of the estate. Keitel had to choose another profession.

He chose a line of work that, like being a landowner, was held in high esteem in Germany, but was at odds with his family's heritage of opposition to the ruling regime. He signed up for the military. It was a decision that would later lead to his execution.

As the Nazis gained political power, many within military leadership saw Adolf Hitler as an incompetent, juvenile hothead who was causing problems. Many top-level military officers tried to figure out how best to assassinate him and take over the government to show the world that not all Germans were like the Nazis. (In 1944, some carried out a plan to do just that, but it failed, leading to thousands of arrests and executions by the Gestapo—the clandestine and cruel Nazi police.) But not Keitel.

After some brief opposition to some of Hitler's decisions and desires, Keitel eventually became supremely loyal to the Führer—so much so that his military colleagues generally viewed him with disgust because he had transformed himself from a respectable general into Hitler's "yes man."[6]

As the Nazi regime implemented its reign of terror, Keitel played an intimate part. As a leader in the military, and at Hitler's direction, he had signed dozens of orders that called for soldiers and political prisoners to be killed or "disappeared." After the war conclud-

ed and top-level Nazi op-
eratives were put on trial for
their war crimes at Nurem-
berg, Keitel admitted that
he knew these orders were
illegal. In a letter to an in-
terrogator for the American
military, he wrote:

> In carrying out these
> thankless and dif-

Wilhelm Keitel with Adolf Hitler

> ficult tasks I had to fulfill my duty under the
> hardest exigencies of war, often acting against
> the inner voice of my conscience and against
> my own convictions. The fulfillment of ur-
> gent tasks assigned by Hitler to whom I was
> directly responsible demanded complete
> self-abnegation.[7]

In his defense, like other Nazi and German military officials charged with committing war crimes,
Keitel aimed to shirk responsibility for what he did by
noting that he was merely following orders. This argument was in line with the *Führerprinzip*, or "leader
principle"—a political argument in Germany at the
time that suggested that all laws and decisions must be
in line with whatever the Führer (Hitler) said. Citing
this line of thinking, Keitel was hoping to be absolved

of the horrific acts he helped implement. He was expecting that the positive laws Hitler set up would override the natural law—murder is always wrong. These hopes and expectations did not materialize; Keitel was sentenced to death by hanging.[8]

Was Keitel wrong to do what he did? What about Abbott? Both men were following orders from other people, in a sense. Abbott was doing what he said God had commanded. Keitel was doing what the Führer had commanded. But their actions are polar opposites; one was helping people, the other was killing people. One was inherently good, though made *illegal*; the other was inherently bad, though made *legal*.

This contrast helps us understand the fundamental question that is the entire purpose of law: to define what is wrong, to prohibit it, and to punish those who do it. To explore the idea further, let's look at two Latin phrases that are commonly used to help explain the two types of "wrong" actions: *malum in se* (wrong in itself) and *malum prohibitum* (wrong because it is prohibited).

MALUM IN SE

For several years, ABC aired a popular game show, *The Dating Game,* in which eager contestants applied from around the country for a chance to appear on TV and perhaps find love along the way. One of the many hopefuls in the 1978 season was a man from California named Rodney Alcala—a man who was quite different from his competitors. Rodney was no ordinary bachelor—he was a convicted felon who had sexually violated a young girl and attempted to murder her.[9]

Despite having served time in prison and being a registered sex offender, ABC allowed Alcala to appear on the show—and he won. The "lucky lady" who picked him for a date, rather than the two other men, ended up refusing to go out with him, calling him "creepy."

She was right. Before the TV appearance, Alcala had killed at least two women in California and two more in New York. His crimes continued in the following years, and while the total body count is unknown, detectives estimate that he abused and killed several dozen of women.[10]

That feeling in your gut? I feel the same as I write these awful words. These horrendous murders shock our senses, and we condemn them. They are actions so awful that they clearly violate our moral code of conduct, and we fully agree that they should be prohibited and punished. This is an example of a *malum in se*—something that's inherently wrong. These actions "violate the natural, moral or public principles of a civilized society."[11] We can readily and easily understand that they are improper behavior.

An action that is *malum in se* (or *mala in se*, plural) is not dependent on a legislator passing a bill to be wrong; killing an innocent person or stealing candy from a child is wrong even if Congress failed to pass a law banning these activities.

Another important point: these types of crimes have a victim who has been harmed by the aggressor. A person is clearly wronged when somebody commits a *malum in se* offense. An innocent person loses his life; a child loses his candy. Victims such as these help us clearly identify when something *wrong* has happened. We don't have to look to a list of laws to interpret whether something bad has happened—we can see it with our own eyes.

As you can tell, these types of offenses pertain to the natural or common law. A society-wide understanding of something being a wrongful act justifies punishing those who commit them. Murder, rape, robbery, burglary, and theft—these types of acts, which have a clear victim, are, therefore, clearly wrong.

Now, things get tricky when the government specifically says that there is no victim—in other words, when politicians legalize the wrongful activity. Every child knows that it's wrong to steal, and that is a clear *malum se*. But then consider a policy called civil asset forfeiture, which literally allows government prosecutors to take people's property without even charging them with a crime. We are supposed to be presumed innocent until we are proven guilty by a government lawyer, so you might think that until that happens, you should be able to keep your property. Think again. Across the country, people have their money, cars, computers, or even homes taken by the government even though they are innocent of any wrongdoing.

It's difficult to imagine that laws like this actually exist. Some might think that even though it's "on the books," the law isn't actually used. That's not at all the case with forfeitures. For example, in 2014—and for the first time ever in American history—federal agents took more property from people than burglars did.[12] Consider just one department within the feder-

Total annual dollar value of assets seized by federal law enforcement and burglary losses

al government that takes property from people without charging them with a crime: the Drug Enforcement Administration (DEA). From 2007 to 2017, the agency seized over $3 billion from people without any judicial review whatsoever—no criminal or civil charges in court. A report of this program by the Inspector General noted that the Department of Justice "does not collect or evaluate the data necessary to know whether its seizures and forfeitures are effective, or the extent to which seizures present potential risks to civil liberties."[13] The federal government is flying blind while scooping up people's property—people like Joseph Rivers.

Joseph Rivers

Rivers had a dream of starting a music video company, and after saying goodbye to his family in Detroit, boarded an Amtrak train to Los Angeles. He brought the $16,000 his friends and family had donated to help him start the business. But he never made it to his destination. At a stop at the Amtrak station in Albuquerque, New Mexico, DEA agents boarded the train and began asking passengers where they were headed and why. When asked, Rivers answered, and when agents requested to search his bags, Rivers agreed. After all, he hadn't done anything wrong; he wasn't accused of breaking a law.[14]

The agents found the money still in the bank envelope; Rivers explained that he was using it to start a new business and that he had trouble in the past withdrawing large amounts of cash from out-of-state banks. The government employees didn't believe him; they suspected that the money was connected to some sort of drug activity. There was no evidence of this—no guns, no drugs, and no information that would suggest such a connection. But that lack of evidence didn't prevent the DEA agents from taking the money. Rivers commented:

> These officers took everything that I had worked so hard to save and even money that was given to me by family that believed in me. I told [the DEA agents] I had no money and no means to survive in Los Angeles if they took my money. They informed me that it was my responsibility to figure out how I was going to do that.[15]

Rivers wasn't arrested or charged with a crime. He simply had his money taken, and his dreams delayed.

Is something that is wrong for you and I to do suddenly permissible because some politicians said it was okay? Recall what Bastiat said: legitimate law is merely the "collective organization of [an] individual right." In other words, government can only do what we can do, if we group together and decide to delegate that power to the government. The definition of *malum in se*—wrong in and of itself—does not have an asterisk attached, explaining in a footnote that the definition does not apply to the government. Something that violates "the natural, moral or public principles of a civilized society" is wrong for you, me, and government employees, too.

MALUM PROHIBITUM

Romaine Quinn was a senior in high school in 2009. Rather than campaigning to be class president, he took it up a notch—he decided to try and win a spot on the city council in Rice Lake, Wisconsin. He won, and only a year later—as a freshman at a nearby university—he was elected to be the mayor, the youngest in the city's history.

Just months into Quinn's service as mayor, the county district attorney filed criminal charges against him.

Quinn had not stolen city money, nor was he elected under false pretenses. He didn't do anything that would be classified as a *malum in se*. His crime was a

$1,609 campaign contribution he had received for his mayoral campaign.

Romaine Quinn

That contribution was properly reported as required under the law. And it wasn't from a shady developer looking to have the new mayor in his pocket, nor was anyone trying to bribe him. The person donating that money was Quinn's own mother.

Neither Quinn nor his mom were aware, it seems, of a Wisconsin statute that limits political contributions. For local races, like the mayoral election in Rice Lake, the cap was $250; his mom had donated over six times that amount. The crime carried a maximum penalty of a $500 fine for Quinn's mom, and he faced another fee of up to $4,800.[16]

Quinn's case is an example of *malum prohibitum* (or *mala prohibita*, plural)—actions that are wrong merely because they have been prohibited. There was nothing inherently wrong with the donation in question, only that it had exceeded an arbitrary limit imposed by the legislature. Would it be "wrong" of Quinn's mom to have donated $251? According to the "law," the answer—based on the fact that it is prohibited, and therefore wrong—is yes.

There are, sadly, an unlimited number of examples to share that illustrate the silliness of thinking something is wrong—and then punishing the person for doing it—merely because it goes against what somebody said should not be allowed. Let's consider a couple more examples to help you see the foolishness in full display.

Mats Järlström

Mats Järlström is a Swedish engineer living in Oregon. One day his wife received a ticket in the mail after she was captured on camera crossing into an intersection after the traffic light had turned red. In response, Järlström created and proposed a new mathematical formula for the traffic cameras to use, which would account for cars slowing down before changing a yellow light to red. "I'm an excellent engineer," he told the Oregon State Board of Examiners for Engineering and Land Surveying.

That statement led the board to impose a $500 fine on him following a two-year investigation. Why? Once again, he hadn't done anything inherently wrong; there was no victim of his math formula on paper. The board was punishing him for calling himself an engineer without their permission. Here is their ruling:

> Järlström applied special knowledge of the mathematical, physical and engineering sciences to such creative work as investigation, evaluation and design in connection with public equipment, processes and works. Järlström thereby engaged in the practice of engineering.[17]

Good thing neither Nikola Tesla nor Leonardo da Vinci lived in Oregon, right? Otherwise, they might have been fined for having the audacity to consider themselves engineers without first obtaining the blessing of the bureaucracy. (These types of laws, called occupational licensure, punish people like Järlström in every state—not just Oregon.)

Before moving on, let's briefly go back to our early lemonade stand example, this time citing a different case. Andre Spicer's 5-year-old daughter wanted to try her hand at selling things to passersby, and after considering toys, food, and clothes, she decided to opt for some easy-to-make lemonade. Each cup was 65 cents, and several happy customers came by to support the budding business. "She brought a smile to their faces," Spicer said of his daughter.[18]

And then the government officials showed up.

Predictably, they pointed out that the girl was selling her lemonade without a commercial license. When confronted with the $200 fine, and seeing that she was somehow in trouble, the young child burst into tears, saying "I've done a bad thing." [19]

Think about that for a moment. A happy girl was selling lemonade to consenting customers, yet she was led to believe that action was somehow wrong. This is the effect of a *malum prohibitum*—when the "law" allows government employees to harass people who are peaceably going about their business.

There are some important things to understand about these so-called "wrongs" before we continue. First, they are entirely dependent upon a positive law; they cannot exist without the government dictating what should not be done and attaching a penalty to it. For example, using our earlier island scenario, imagine in that government-free world that you needed to catch some fish to eat. You'd fashion a pole, line, and lure, and get to work—never thinking to stop and ask everybody else's permission first. Yet chances are the government where you live makes you obtain a fishing license before heading to the lake—only because some politicians decided to pass that law, suddenly making fishing without a license a *malum prohibitum*.

Second, unlike in cases of a *malum in se*, there are no victims. Romaine Quinn getting more than $250 for his mayoral campaign did not harm anyone. Mats Järl-ström's math formula did not hurt those he showed it to. And Andre Spicer's daughter did not lace her lemonade with poison. These actions—violations of positive law—are so-called "victimless crimes." There is no readily identifiable harm caused by such actions.

Third, *malum prohibitum* laws are disconnected from any moral determination; the classical "right and wrong" arguments are cast aside in favor of merely prohibiting whatever politicians don't like or feel is not ideal. Put differently, natural law is ignored and only positive law is used. And worse, this approach leads to punishing people not just for doing certain things, but also for *not* doing something—as in the case of the federal law that punishes people for failing to purchase health care insurance.

Another important point to understand is that a *malum prohibitum* requires knowing about the prohibition. Remember the case with Judge Tucker? "No man's life, liberty, or property are safe while the legislature is in session," he wrote. This is because every time a group of legislators get together, or a president begins signing executive orders, or bureaucrats pass their regulations, we might find ourselves classified as criminals without knowing it; we might not be aware of some new regulation or mandate that affects our lives or limits our actions. A *malum in se* is readily observable and inherently understood; we all know it's wrong to hurt people and take their stuff. But when your action might be deemed wrong merely because some people hundreds or thousands of miles away had a meeting and decided they didn't want you to do it, how are you supposed to suddenly know that you should stop?

Did you know that America's prisons are packed? The USA has the highest prison population in the world: 716 prisoners per 100,000 residents.[20] It might be hard to make sense of that number—how does it compare to other countries? Actually, it's more than five times higher than most of the countries in the world. The United States has roughly five percent of the world's population but has close to 25 percent of the world's prisoners.[21]

Why the difference, then? Why are over two million Americans locked up behind bars?[22]

Part of the answer is because of *mala prohibita*— the result of prohibiting all sorts of actions that don't have victims. Recall that Congress creates an average of 55 new crimes each year, to say nothing of all the regulatory prohibitions that bureaucrats are constantly creating. Nobody knows how many crimes even exist nowadays, as pointed out in one report:

The Congressional Research Service reportedly has been unable to come up with a definitive total of federal criminal laws; the nearest they could come was to say they number in the thousands. They are by no means confined to the federal criminal code—Title 18, itself a weighty volume—but are scattered among the laws contained in the 51 titles or subject-matter volumes of the federal code and the hundreds of thousands of regulations that are supposed to implement those laws. The result is that there are more criminal laws than anyone could know.[23]

Add onto that lengthy list the many state laws that criminalize victimless behavior. In Arizona, "No person shall feed garbage to swine without first obtaining a permit."[24] In Massachusetts it's a crime to play only part of the "Star Spangled Banner"; the law states it must be played "as a whole and separate composition or number, without embellishment or addition in the way of national or other melodies."[25] If you're a pinball player in Arkansas, beware: a "coin-operated amusement device" may provide you "not more than twenty-five (25) free games" without running afoul of the law.[26] And if for some strange reason you find yourself at a New Hampshire beach at night, do not "carry away or collect for the purpose of carrying away any seaweed or rockweed from the seashore," because that is also illegal.[27]

While these silly statutes are clearly *mala prohibita*, they are often not prosecuted; there is no influx of inmates into prison over seaweed collection. A large portion of the prison population is there due to controlled substance violations—the "war on drugs." In the four decades since Richard Nixon started this war (one that has not decreased drug use[28]), the rate of putting people in prison has expanded by 500%.[29] Crime and drug use have not increased, so that doesn't explain the trend. What *has* changed are the laws punishing this activity—longer punishments, mandatory minimums, and other punishments enacted by legislators wanting to be "tough on crime."

Roughly half of America's two million prisoners are there because they allegedly used or sold drugs.[30] But think about it: every drug these people consumed or traded was once legal. These drugs may be harmful (but so are guns, knives, cars, matches, bathroom cleaners, and more), and it is unwise to abuse any substance—no question there. But on the island without a government, you're free to ingest something that hurts you. That would be a bad idea, but go ahead—knock yourself out. Yet in our day, positive laws prohibit consumption of certain drugs, and even though this activity was once legal, suddenly it became illegal—a *malum prohibitum*—putting hundreds of thousands of people behind bars.

Is that justice?

MENS REA

Continuing with the drug example, let's look at Abby McLean's story to discuss *intent*—whether a person knew their action was "wrong" and decided to do it anyway. McLean was a 28-year-old stay-at-home mom in Colorado when, returning home to her children one night in 2014, she came upon a DUI checkpoint where police officers were stopping all drivers to find impaired drivers who might be a danger on the road.

Abby Mclean

Though a regular user of cannabis (marijuana), McLean was not driving intoxicated. "I hadn't drank [*sic*] or smoked anything, so I was like, 'Let's go through the checkpoint,'" she recalled in an interview.

But the police officer who began asking her questions claimed that McLean's eyes were bloodshot and that he could smell cannabis coming from the car.

So he took out the handcuffs, and McLean freaked out: "Like, massive panic attack. And, 'Oh, my God, I have babies at home. I need to get home. I can't go to jail!'"

McLean's blood test revealed that she had five times the legal limit of tetrahydrocannabinol (THC), the psychoactive part of cannabis—except, she wasn't pulled over for speeding, swerving, or anything that would demonstrate that she was actually an impaired driver. All the police and prosecutor knew was that she had the metabolite in her system—basically, a broken-down part of the cannabis that sticks around in your body for a while.[31]

And that's the problem. Consider alcohol, which is what most people think of when talking about impaired driving. Alcohol is water soluble, meaning that it can be digested rather rapidly in your body and through your bloodstream. It passes quickly—depending on the amount the person drank, within just a few hours. If it's detectable in your body, then chances are you're still being impaired by it.

But THC sticks around for a long time—up to several weeks or more. That's because it's not water soluble; it gets stored in your body's fat cells. That means a person can consume cannabis in a state where it's legal, and then a month later drive around in a state where it's not, and if they are pulled over and suspected of any wrongdoing, they can be prosecuted for DUI—driving under the influence. All the police officer has to do is run a blood, saliva, or urine test to find the metabolite, even though it is not impairing the person at all.

That's why McLean got in trouble. She didn't do anything wrong, but she violated a law that prohibited operating a vehicle while having a drug metabolite in her body. More to the point, she did not know about this law—who does? Unsuspecting people might ingest cannabis in a location where it's legal, only to find themselves classified as a criminal while driving to work weeks later in a location where it's illegal, even though, by then, they are completely sober.

This is where *mens rea* becomes very important. It's Latin for "guilty mind," and refers to a person's mental state when committing an action. McLean did not have a guilty mind—criminal intent—because she wasn't even aware of this law and was intentionally sober while driving her car, hoping to return home to her young children. She was not purposefully intoxicated while driving—she wasn't intoxicated at all.

Mens rea is an important element that any crime should contain before the alleged criminal is convicted. And it applies to both a *malum in se* and *malum prohibitum*. Let's briefly explore why.

The easiest example to point to is the worst of the worst: murder. The premeditated planning to end someone's life is a clearly wrongful act, whether or not a law exists to punish it. It violates the other person's right to life. And because a murderer plans and executes this intentional killing, he definitely has *mens rea*—a guilty mind. But if this element is missing—if the killer did not previously plan to end the person's life—then he likely can't be convicted of murder. He would probably instead be charged with manslaughter, a lesser crime, and would, potentially, be found innocent depending on whether it was an accident or the result of something the person could not have foreseen or did not know.

Blake Layman

The importance of *mens rea* is illustrated in the following example, where a person was accused of felony murder despite not killing anyone. As a 16-year-old, Blake Layman and four of his friends stupidly decided to break into a man's house, unarmed, to rob him of whatever they might find. That homeowner, Rodney Scott, opened fire on the intruders, killing one of them. The others were arrested. A few hours later, Layman was informed that he was being charged with murder.

"I was shell-shocked," he later told a reporter. "Felony murder? That's the first I'd heard of it. How could it be murder when I didn't kill anyone?"[32] He and his friends were not armed, and therefore did not fire a single shot—they were the ones on the receiving end of the barrage of bullets. But that didn't matter. As it turns out, several states have laws that allow a person to be charged with murder if a death occurred while they were committing a felony (a serious crime, such as breaking and entering into a person's home to rob them).

Layman didn't intend to harm, let alone kill, the man whose home they were invading. He certainly didn't intend to kill his friend who died of a gunshot wound. If Layman did not have that mindset, then he should not be able to be convicted of that crime. Prosecutors and judges throughout the process disagreed, and Layman faced 50 years in prison after he and his friends were convicted by a jury for felony murder. Eventually, the Indiana State Supreme Court overturned the conviction, noting that there was a lack of "dangerously violent and threatening conduct"—in other words, *mens rea*—indicating they wanted somebody to die that night. Layman was re-sentenced on a burglary charge only, with 10 years of prison. He was released after three and a half years of prison time and is now a free man—one who, hopefully, has learned from his youthful mistakes.

Demonstrating a criminal mindset to convict a person as a criminal is also important in *malum prohibitum* cases. Again, the explosion of new crimes involving actions that aren't inherently wrong provides many examples:

- In 2007, the Sackett family began loading their new property in Idaho with dirt and rocks so they could build a house. Shortly after they began, the Environmental Protection Agency sent them a notice indicating they were on protected wetlands and had violated the Clean Water Act by altering their land without first obtaining a permit. Unaware their land was under such a designation, they faced tens of thousands of dollars in fines if they failed to remove the dirt and restore the property back to its original state.[33]

- Using the popular Airbnb service, Stephen Palmer and his family rented out their basement, unaware that they were violating the city's law prohibiting them from doing so. Despite the fact that the mayor, who lived two doors down, was completely unaware of the guests coming and going from the home without any noise or controversy, the city threatened Palmer with up to 90 days in jail and heavy fines.[34]

- Robert Eldridge, a fisherman, accidentally trapped a humpback whale in his fishing net near Cape Cod in 2008. He wasn't able to untangle the net, but by cutting the fishing line Eldridge freed the whale, which swam away. This action evidently violated the Endangered Species Act and the Marine Mammal Protection Act, which Eldridge did not realize; he was fined $500 and told that under the law he should have called a licensed marine mammal rescue worker instead of fixing the problem himself.[35]

- Maisha Joefield, a single mom, took a relaxing bath one evening after putting her 5-year-old daughter to sleep. After the bath, she checked on her daughter, but the girl was missing. She frantically searched the apartment and couldn't find her. Then the police showed up. The young girl had gone across the street to her great-grandmother's house—a place she knew she could go in an emergency. But police officers charged Joefield with "endangering the welfare of a child" and placed her in jail. The girl was put in foster care.[36]

- In a hurry to catch a bus one morning in 2010, Oregon resident Scott Miller crossed the street in the middle of the block—not at a designated crosswalk. An observant law enforcement officer detained Miller, began to handcuff him, and tackled him to the ground. Miller was arrested, held at the precinct for 30 minutes, and given a ticket for jaywalking. Needless to say, he missed his bus.[37]

"No problem," you might say in response to some of these stories. "If I'm ever arrested for one of these *malum prohibitum* laws, I'll just say that I wasn't aware of the law. How can I be held accountable for what some group of politicians decides to pass into law, if I don't even know about it?"

You'd be wrong. Whether you are aware of what the government does or not, you're still held responsible for it. Remember: *Ignorantia juris non excusat* ("ignorance of the law is no excuse"). Even if you are unaware of the *malum prohibitum* law you violate, the government won't care. You'll be guilty just the same.

And that's why *mens rea* is so important. The government should first have to establish that you had a guilty mindset—that you both *knew* about the law and *purposefully intended* to violate it. This would protect individuals who have accidentally or unknowingly broken the law because if the law is not easily understood or readily apparent, as in the case of *malum in se* laws, it's unreasonable to punish them.

NOTES

1. Hannah Arendt, *The Life of the Mind: The Groundbreaking Investigation on How We Think* (San Diego: Harcourt, 1981), 13.
2. Mike Clary, "Homeless Advocate, 90, Gets World Attention as Fort Lauderdale Tries to Stop His Outdoor Feedings," *Fort Lauderdale (FL) Sun Sentinel*, November 9, 2014, http://www.sun-sentinel.com/local/broward/fort-lauderdale/fl-homeless-advocate-abbot-profile-20141107-story.html.
3. Kevin Conlon and Catherine E. Shoichet, "90-year-old Florida Man Charged for Feeding Homeless People," CNN, November 5, 2014, http://www.cnn.com/2014/11/04/justice/florida-feeding-homeless-charges/index.html.
4. Peter Holley, "After 90-year-old Is Arrested, Florida Judge Halts Law That Restricts Feeding the Homeless," *Washington Post*, December 3, 2014, https://www.washingtonpost.com/news/post-nation/wp/2014/12/03/after-90-year-old-is-arrested-florida-judge-halts-law-that-restricts-feeding-the-homeless/.
5. "90-year-old Florida Man Charged for Feeding Homeless People," CNN.
6. Samuel W. Mitcham, *The Rise of the Wehrmacht*, vol. 1 (Westport: Praeger Security International, 2008), 107-8.
7. Gene Mueller, *The Forgotten Field Marshal, Wilhelm Keitel* (Durham, NC: Moore Publishing, 1979), 342.
8. Walter Gorlitz, ed., *The Memoirs of Field-Marshal Wilhelm Keitel, Chief of the German High Command, 1938-1945* (New York: Cooper Square Press, 2000).
9. Michael Winter, "Serial Killer Was 'Dating Game' Winner in '78, During Spree," *USA Today*, March 8, 2010, http://content.usatoday.com/communities/ondeadline/post/2010/03/

   serial-killer-alcala-was-dating-game-winner-in-78-dur-
   ing-spree/.

10. Greg Mellen, "Serial Killer Rodney Alcala Charged
   in Slaying of Pregnant Woman in Wyoming," *Orange
   County Register (CA)*, September 21, 2016, http://
   www.ocregister.com/2016/09/21/serial-killer-rodney-
   alcala-charged-in-slaying-of-pregnant-woman-in-wyo-
   ming/.

11. *The People's Law Dictionary*, s.v. "malum in se," http://
   dictionary.law.com/Default.aspx?selected=1201.

12. Christopher Ingraham, "Law Enforcement Took
   More Stuff from People Than Burglars Did Last Year,"
   Washington Post, November 23, 2015, https://www.
   washingtonpost.com/news/wonk/wp/2015/11/23/
   cops-took-more-stuff-from-people-than-burglars-did-
   last-year/.

13. Christopher Ingraham, "Since 2007, the DEA Has
   Taken $3.2 Billion in Cash from People Not Charged
   with a Crime," *Washington Post*, March 29, 2017,
   https://www.washingtonpost.com/news/wonk/
   wp/2017/03/29/since-2007-the-dea-has-taken-3-2-bil-
   lion-in-cash-from-people-not-charged-with-a-crime/.

14. Joline Krueger, "DEA to Traveler: Thanks, I'll Take That
   Cash," *Albuquerque Journal*, May 6, 2015, https://www.
   abqjournal.com/580107/dea-agents-seize-16000-from-
   aspiring-music-video-producer.html.

15. Ibid.

16. "Area Mayor Faces Fine for Accepting Illegal Campaign
   Contribution," WREX, October 6, 2010, http://www.
   wrex.com/story/13278325/area-mayor-could-be-
   fined-for-accepting-illegal-campaign-contribution.

17. Steven Nelson, "Man Fined $500 for Criticizing Traffic
   Cameras with Math," *U.S. News and World Report*,
   April 26, 2017, https://www.usnews.com/news/arti-
   cles/2017-04-26/man-fined-500-for-criticizing-traffic-
   cameras-with-math.

18. Kim Hjelmgaard, "'I've done a bad thing,' Says British Girl, 5, Fined for Selling Lemonade," *Spectrum*, July 21, 2017, http://www.thespectrum.com/story/news/world/2017/07/21/british-girl-5-fined-selling-lemonade-united-kingdom/498680001/.

19. Ibid.

20. Michelle Ye Hee Lee, "Yes, U.S. Locks People Up at a Higher Rate Than Any Other Country," *Washington Post*, July 7, 2015, https://www.washingtonpost.com/news/fact-checker/wp/2015/07/07/yes-u-s-locks-people-up-at-a-higher-rate-than-any-other-country/.

21. Michelle Ye Hee Lee, "Does the United States Really Have 5 Percent of the World's Population and One Quarter of the World's Prisoners?," *Washington Post*, April 30, 2015, https://www.washingtonpost.com/news/fact-checker/wp/2015/04/30/does-the-united-states-really-have-five-percent-of-worlds-population-and-one-quarter-of-the-worlds-prisoners/.

22. "Incarceration," Sentencing Project, http://www.sentencingproject.org/issues/incarceration/.

23. Paul Larkin and Michael Mukasey, "The Perils of Overcriminalization," Heritage Foundation, February 12, 2015, http://www.heritage.org/report/the-perils-overcriminalization.

24. AZ Rev Stat § 3-2664 (1996 through 1st Reg Sess 50th Legis).

25. National Anthem; Manner of Playing, Massachusetts Code, § IV-1-264-9.

26. Pinball machines, etc, AR Code, § 5-66-111 (2012).

27. Collecting Seaweed, New Hampshire code, Section 207:48 (effective Nov. 1, 1973).

28. Eduardo Porter, "Numbers Tell of Failure in Drug War," *New York Times*, July 3, 2012, http://www.nytimes.com/2012/07/04/business/in-rethinking-the-war-on-drugs-start-with-the-numbers.html.

29. "Criminal Justice Facts," Sentencing Project, http://www.sentencingproject.org/criminal-justice-facts/.

30. Kathleen Miles, "Just How Much The War on Drugs Impacts Our Overcrowded Prisons, in One Chart," *Huffington Post*, March 10, 2014, http://www.huffingtonpost.com/2014/03/10/war-on-drugs-prisons-infographic_n_4914884.html.

31. Ben Markus and Stephanie O'Neill, "The Difficulty of Enforcing Laws against Driving While High," NPR, September 6, 2016, http://www.npr.org/sections/health-shots/2016/09/06/492810932/the-difficulty-of-enforcing-laws-against-driving-while-high.

32. Ed Pilkington, "Felony Murder: Why a Teenager Who Didn't Kill Anyone Faces 55 Years in Jail," *Guardian*, February 25, 2015, https://www.theguardian.com/us-news/2015/feb/26/felony-murder-teenager-55-years-jail-indiana.

33. Joan Biskupic, "High Court Weighs High-Profile Case Over Wetlands, EPA Fines," *USA Today*, January 10, 2012, https://usatoday30.usatoday.com/news/washington/judicial/story/2012-01-09/epa-wetlands-scotus-court/52471646/1.

34. "St. George Shutting Down Airbnb Providers," Libertas Institute, May 26, 2015, http://libertasutah.org/interview/st-george-shutting-down-airbnb-providers/.

35. "Chatham Fisherman Who Freed Whale Fined," *Cape Cod Times*, October 1, 2009.

36. Stephanie Clifford and Jessica Silver-Greenberg, "Foster Care as Punishment: The New Reality of 'Jane Crow'," *New York Times*, July 21, 2017, https://www.nytimes.com/2017/07/21/nyregion/foster-care-nyc-jane-crow.html.

37. Helen Jung, "Jaywalking Arrest: Portland Police Did Not Violate SW Portland Man's Constitutional Rights, Judge Says," *Oregonian (Portland, OR)*, January 30, 2014, http://www.oregonlive.com/portland/index.ssf/2014/01/jaywalking_arrest_portland_pol.html.

"The most improper job of any man... is bossing other men. Not one in a million is fit for it, and least of all those who seek the opportunity."[1]

J.R.R. Tolkien

WHO'S IN CHARGE?

One of the funniest satires about government comes from the film *Monty Python and the Holy Grail*. In this cult classic, King Arthur is on a quest to recruit some knights to join his court at Camelot. Arthur finds some peasants working in a field, and hopes to learn the identity of the knight who occupies the nearby castle. Here's a portion of their exchange:

> ARTHUR: How do you do, good lady. I am Arthur, King of the Britons. Whose castle is that?
>
> WOMAN: King of the who?
>
> ARTHUR: The Britons.
>
> WOMAN: Who are the Britons?

King Arthur and the peasants in Monty Python and the Holy Grail

ARTHUR: Well, we all are. We're all Britons and I am your king.

WOMAN: I didn't know we had a king. I thought we were an autonomous collective.

DENNIS: You're fooling yourself. We're living in a dictatorship: a self-perpetuating autocracy in which the working classes-- ...

ARTHUR: Please, please good people. I am in haste. Who lives in that castle?

WOMAN: No one lives there.

ARTHUR: Then who is your lord?

WOMAN: We don't have a lord.

ARTHUR: What?

DENNIS: I told you. We're an anarcho-syndicalist commune. We take it in turns to act as a sort of executive officer for the week.

ARTHUR: Yes...

DENNIS: But all the decisions of that officer have to be ratified at a special biweekly meeting.

ARTHUR: Yes, I see.

DENNIS: By a simple majority in the case of purely internal affairs-- ...

ARTHUR: Be quiet! I order you to be quiet!

WOMAN: Order, eh? Who does he think he is?

ARTHUR: I am your king!

WOMAN: Well, I didn't vote for you.

ARTHUR: You don't vote for kings.

WOMAN: Well, how did you become king then?

ARTHUR [as angels begin singing]: The Lady of the Lake, her arm clad in the purest shimmering samite, held aloft Excalibur from the bosom of the water signifying by Divine Providence that I, Arthur, was to carry Excalibur. *That* is why I am your king!

DENNIS: Listen. Strange women lying in ponds distributing swords is no basis for a system of government. Supreme executive power derives from a mandate from the masses, not from some farcical aquatic ceremony.

ARTHUR: Be quiet!

DENNIS: Well you can't expect to wield supreme executive power just 'cause some watery tart threw a sword at you!

ARTHUR: Shut up!

DENNIS: I mean, if I went around sayin' I was an emperor just because some moistened bint had lobbed a scimitar at me they'd put me away!

ARTHUR: Shut up! Will you shut up![2]

What of a monarchy, as in Arthur's case? Does "holding aloft Excalibur" entitle a person to rule over others? Does being born to the previous king?

What of an "anarcho-syndicalist commune," which the peasant Dennis described? Does rotating authority among peers work? Or is majority rule the right way to decide issues and determine what the law should be?

Or how about what America has (at least in theory): a constitutional republic. Does having a Constitution justify whatever Congress wants to do? Should we submit to whatever the government dictates, merely because we have elections and the so-called "rule of law"?

In the previous chapters, we addressed various forms of law and what types of laws legitimately punish wrongful activity. Once we establish *what* is wrong, we must then determine *who* can do something about it—who recognizes these laws, creates them, and enforces them. Put differently, we need to understand what forms of government are acceptable to prohibit and punish wrongdoing.

Think back to the island scenario. Let's say one of your neighbors decides to impose a monarchy on the rest of you and claims ownership over the island, but then he leaves you alone, doesn't tax you, and you rarely see him. (Unlikely, right?) Or consider a scenario where all of the island's inhabitants vote on whether to create a representative democracy and elect a president. This happens, and you're put in charge—but then you leave everybody alone to go about their business. These forms of government, then, don't matter as much as what those in government *actually do*. If you and everybody else adhered to natural law and only punished *malum in se* actions—violations of natural law—it wouldn't matter if there was a king or a president. Here's how Bastiat explains it:

> If a nation were founded on this basis [of natural law], it seems to me that order would prevail among the people, in thought as well as in deed. It seems to me that such a nation would have the most simple, easy to accept, economi-

cal, limited, non-oppressive, just, and enduring government imaginable—whatever its political form might be.[3]

Unfortunately, this utopia has to remain only "imaginable," since the world is littered with governments that aren't founded on that basis. They don't leave people alone. They tax. They take. They assume all sorts of new powers and punish an expanding list of *malum prohibitum* activities.

While many good things can come from legitimate government activity—imprisoning murderers, repelling an invasion, punishing thieves, etc.—the concentration of political power creates many problems as well. Governments of all sizes and shapes have been the instruments of destruction in the lives of their subjects. They too easily turn justice into injustice, violating the very purpose for which they exist. Rather than protecting, they harm.

Dennis the peasant was right: a person should not be able to have power over others because they are given a sword. But is a person entitled to this power for other reasons, such as winning a popularity contest (also known as an election)?

What type of government can have legitimate authority over you?

CREATOR AND CREATURE

Lest you think other-
wise, let me make some-
thing clear: not everybody is
a fan of natural law. One of
its critics was a man named
Jeremy Bentham, who called
it "nonsense upon stilts."[4]
Bentham was an eighteenth-
century English philosopher
and social reformer who be-

Jeremy Bentham

lieved that actions—and laws—should be evaluated not
on their moral implications, but on their consequences.
This concept, known as utilitarianism, measures what
is right or wrong based on "the greatest happiness of
the greatest number" of people. This, he argued, was
"the only right and justifiable end of government."[5]

In other words, Bentham believed that the purpose
of government was to improve the lives of the most
people possible—good ends would justify whatever
means were used to obtain them. You might wonder, as
I do, whether the happiness of the majority of people is
a praiseworthy result if it is achieved by hurting the minority of people. If 51% of people in a country would be
most happy by taking half of the money and belongings

of the other 49%, is there anything wrong with that? If law is not connected to morality, then does it matter if some people are disadvantaged by the law? Some will be peasants and some will be kings and knights—and that's okay in this way of thinking, as long as the privileged politicians and their friends are happy.

This dangerous idea was further refined by one of Bentham's students, John Austin, the British legal theorist mentioned earlier who championed positive law. A professor of jurisprudence at the University of London, Austin refined and propagated these ideas even further. How did he do it? Well, how would you do it? If you're a utilitarian and you wish to govern a society based only on the merits of the outcomes of each law or action, what type of government would you need? Where would the authority come from in such a scheme?

Austin argued that "every political society must have a sovereign... freed from legal restraints." In other words, the government and its officers should be exempted from any negative legal consequences for their actions. Those in government should not be "constrained to observe [the law] by any legal sanction," or punishment. But why a separate set of rules for the government versus those who are governed by this group of people? Because if the government had to follow its own rules, Austin wrote, it "would be in a state of subjection," rather than sovereign, or supreme.[6]

Surely your mind begins spinning at the thought of letting the government get away with whatever it wants. This sounds like something out of a dystopian novel. But Austin was very influential in the decades that followed, and modern governments implement the very thing he championed.

Ever heard of *sovereign immunity*? It's the idea that government can do no wrong and cannot be sued by those who have been harmed by its actions. This idea dates back to the early monarchy in England, where kings could not be sued in their own courts. Think of it: these kings did some pretty horrible things, and if their subjects could hold them accountable in court, as one historian said, the monarchs "would have passed [their lives] as defendant,"[7] continually fighting off lawsuits. From this immunity developed the idea of *rex non potest peccare*, meaning "the king can do no wrong." Initially, this concept referred directly to the individual serving as king, and not to the government per se. Here's how Blackstone explained it:

> Besides the attribute of sovereignty, the law also ascribes to the king in his political capacity absolute perfection. The king can do no wrong....
>
> The king, moreover, is not only incapable of doing wrong, but even of thinking wrong: he can never mean to do an improper thing: in him is no folly or weakness.[8]

Eventually, the idea of *personal* immunity held by the king was merged into *political* immunity. It wasn't just that the king could do no wrong, but that the government in general held the same status. And this idea, which Austin helped refine and popularize, spread to the American colonists—former British subjects themselves. Sovereign immunity persisted through the creation of the Constitution. Alexander Hamilton, writing in *Federalist* No. 81, said, "It is inherent in the nature of sovereignty, not to be amenable [subject] to the [law]suit of an individual *without its consent*."[9] James Madison agreed: "It is not in the power of individuals to call any state into court."[10] And John Marshall, the first chief justice of the U.S. Supreme Court, echoed this sentiment: "It is not rational to suppose that the sovereign power should be dragged before a court."[11]

These defenders of the newly formed government rightly argued that the proposed federal government was a creation of the states. The states, each one a sovereign nation, had been freed from British rule. Each was named and recognized individually in the peace treaty that followed the war. And these states, or nation states, sent delegates to create a new compact—a new government that would remedy the perceived problems under the Articles of Confederation that had been in operation for a few years. The federal government did not create the states; it was they that first existed, and then they got together to organize and empower this new federal government. It was intended to be a creature of the states, and they were its creators.

But what are the states themselves? Many consider them "sovereign," but what then of you and me? Are *we* not sovereign? Are we in charge of ourselves—free and independent people? Or are we creatures of the state, subject to whatever the state decides?

Let's ask this a different way. If the federal government is a creature of the states, then who created the states? Recall our island example and the organization of a new government. That government—a "state," if you wish to call it that—can only have the powers that the islanders already have themselves and then choose to delegate to it. They create the government. They are the creators; it is the creature.

But our island example doesn't exemplify today's political climate. States have been around longer than you or me. Most states were basically created by the federal government after purchasing or seizing land from other people. Even the early states, originating as colonies, often began as royal charters—government with permission of the king. So the theory breaks down in modern reality, where the state is basically its own entity, separate and apart from the people it rules. It may feel nice to say that it should only have the powers that we have and delegate to it, but centuries of court cases and legal practice are at odds with this theory. They are sovereign. They are both creator and creature, in a way. Confusing, right?

The takeaway here is that government tends to treat its citizens as peasants, and it perceives itself as did King Arthur: entitled to authority, derived from some unseen, mystical source, never questioning the right to rule and to wield power. It's good to be king, especially when everybody believes you "can do no wrong."

SOCIETY AND THE STATE

Alexis de Tocqueville

Ever heard of Alexis de Tocqueville? He was a French political scientist who visited America in 1831 on an official mission to examine prisons and learn about incarceration reforms. But he had a sneaky reason for requesting this opportunity to visit the New World.

Tocqueville wasn't nearly as interested in prisons as he was in American society itself. He wanted to study the religious, political, and economic character of the new nation. His results were later published in *Democracy in America*, a two-volume set of books cataloging his many observations.

Keep in mind where Tocqueville came from. Europe was a product of centuries of conflict, conquest, and corruption. Monarchies were everywhere, and individuals were treated as subjects, not as free people. Freedom was granted by government, not inherent or pre-existing. And whenever a problem arose, the citizenry looked to the government for a solution. "Wherever at the head of some new undertaking you see the government in France, or a man of rank in England," Tocqueville wrote, "in the United States you will be sure to find an association"—a voluntary group of people. He continued:

> Americans of all ages, all conditions, and all dispositions constantly form associations. They have not only commercial and manufacturing companies, in which all take part, but associations of a thousand other kinds, religious, moral, serious, futile, general or restricted, enormous or diminutive. The Americans make associations to give entertainments, to found seminaries, to build inns, to construct churches, to diffuse books, to send missionaries to the antipodes; in this manner they found hospitals, prisons, and

schools. If it is proposed to inculcate some truth or to foster some feeling by the encouragement of a great example, they form a society.[12]

The Frenchman was intrigued by these spontaneous organizations designed to solve problems. "I have often admired," he added, "the extreme skill with which the inhabitants of the United States succeed in proposing a common object for the exertions of a great many men and in inducing them voluntarily to pursue it."[13] Government didn't need to tax people and pay others to do large projects. Early Americans were voluntarily doing similar things themselves.

While the America Tocqueville described has largely faded into history, his writings raise an important distinction we should consider as we explore the idea of governmental authority. Too often, people confuse society and the state, leading to the elimination of the role society can—and should—play in providing for the needs of individuals.

What is society? The word comes from the Latin *societas*, meaning a fellowship, association, alliance, or community. When you go to a grocery store, amusement park, church, or community theater, you see society—groups of people going about their business, often in a shared experience. Other voluntary associations might be formed to clean up the neighborhood, help save whales, share best practices in an industry, publish inspirational stories, or help parents connect with one another. As Tocqueville observed, the sky's the limit; any problem in need of a solution could be helped through a group of people organizing together to take it on.

Society requires voluntary association; to force someone to join an association is to enslave a person. If my elderly neighbor is unable to mow her lawn, some friends and I might associate together to take turns weekly to get the job done. But if the city council compels us to mow her lawn under threat of fines or jail time, then our effort is no longer an association—ours is not a "fellowship" or "alliance." Consenting to join an association requires us to agree, so society is really just a mental concept—a decision by individuals to share something in common together. This means that society can only really exist if individuals freely choose to act with one another.

You may wonder, then, whether the state qualifies as an association. Here we're not talking about American "states" like Georgia or Nevada, but a general term often used by some to describe the government, though they aren't truly synonymous. Your city is "the state," as is Canada, the Democratic People's Republic of Korea, and Funkley, Minnesota (popula-

Murray Rothbard

tion: five). The state is a political organization that has two unique characteristics: it uses coercion and violence, and it claims jurisdiction (authority) over a specific, defined territory. Murray Rothbard, a prolific economist and historian, explains this concept further:

> While other individuals or institutions obtain their income by production of goods and services and by the peaceful and voluntary sale of these goods and services to others, the state obtains its revenue by the use of compulsion; that is, by the use and the threat of the jailhouse and the bayonet. Having used force and violence to obtain its revenue, the state generally goes on to regulate and dictate the other actions of its individual subjects.[14]

These subjects are anyone who happens to live in a geographical boundary over which the state claims authority, be it a city, a "state," or a country. If you don't do what the state's officials say while living within their territory, you will be punished. They might start lightly—a fine, community service, etc.—but if you defy their authority and refuse to submit, the consequences will escalate, leading potentially to your imprisonment or even death.

This sounds like a gang, doesn't it? You're minding your own business when suddenly a group with guns comes up to you and demands some of your money, which they say will be used to help protect you. "I don't need your protection," you might reply. "Too bad," the gang would say. "This is our neighborhood now." And, like the state, you would likely submit to the gang, calculating that it's in your best interest to just do what they say and hope they leave you alone as much as possible.

Rothbard also referred to the state as "the systematization of the predatory process over a given territory."[15] Here, predatory means attacking or stealing from others, like a predator does to its prey. But the state wouldn't exist for very long if its subjects perceive it as a gang or a predator. What inevitably happens, then, is that the state becomes a participatory process, where the subjects have a say in choosing who their rulers (or predators) will be. The state is a creation of their own making—or at least citizens feel that way when they cast their vote.

So where does the confusion come from—why do people not distinguish more clearly between society and the state? One is voluntary, the other is not. One uses persuasion, the other coercion. Pretty simple, right?

The problem arises when people want something to be done in society but prefer not to help bring it about themselves. "There ought to be a law," some will say. "Poor people need help." Vague statements such as these lead people to support policies that bring about a desired result—shelter for the homeless, food for the needy, health care for the unemployed, etc. But such policies require compulsion; rather than forming an association to deal with the problem, these individuals turn to the state.

This is socialism—basically, a mixing of society and the state. In other words, the state is used to bring about social (or society-wide) objectives. More trees should be planted? Sure, the government can take care of that. People want a park? Okay, the government will step in and provide. In these cases, the costs of each government program or expense are socialized—they are spread out across everybody in society. What happens, then, is that the cost becomes so small for each person that they feel the program is "worth it." Funding public schools, building a new road, constructing a new police station, putting on a parade—these and a host of other activities are state programs, but the costs are dispersed over many people. Each expense is so minimal that it doesn't feel very burdensome on its own—until you look at your total tax burden, perhaps.

Bastiat had something to say about this. He pointed out, as mentioned above, that socialism "confuses the distinction between [the state] and society." Because of this, "every time we object to a thing being done by [the state], the socialists conclude that we object to its being done at all."[16] In other words, if you were to oppose using taxes to fund schools, socialists would say that you must not want children to be educated at all. Bastiat destroyed that argument:

> We disapprove of state education. Then the socialists say that we are opposed to any education. We object to a state religion. Then the socialists say that we want no religion at all. We object to a state-enforced equality. Then they say that we are against equality. And so on, and so on. It is as if the socialists were to accuse us of not wanting persons to eat because we do not want the state to raise grain.[17]

The danger with using the state to serve society's needs, rather than voluntary associations, is that if people stop working together, and instead turn to a third party (the state), we weaken the bonds that tie us together. Society is undermined and ultimately destroyed.

In summarizing his observations, Tocqueville wrote:

> Among the laws that rule human societies there is one which seems to be more precise and clear than all others. If men are to remain civilized or to become so, the art of associating together must grow and improve in the same ratio in which the equality of conditions is increased.[18]

Ask yourself, now that you've read his description of early America: in our day, has this art of associating improved? Are we better at voluntarily working together to achieve important societal goals? If not, then what is happening to our society, and how do we push back against the growth of the state?

CONSENT OF THE GOVERNED

The Declaration of Independence contains an important phrase many people overlook: "governments... deriv[e] their just powers from the consent of the governed." Consent is the crucial foundation of any legitimate government. To have and use "just (or legitimate) powers," a government must have consent. What does this word mean?

While the definition of consent hasn't changed since the Declaration was written, I find it's helpful to use a dictionary that reflects the understanding of words when they were written. For that we turn to Noah Webster, a man who learned 26 languages to help him compile a dictionary to standardize American English over the course of two decades. Here's how he defined consent in 1828:

> 1. Agreement of the mind to what is proposed or stated by another; accord; hence, a yielding of the mind or will to that which is proposed.

> 2. Accord of minds; agreement; unity of opinion.[19]

Makes sense, right? This is what we think of when we think of consent. So taking it back to the Declaration, we might instead say that governments derive their just powers from the *agreement* of the governed—a yielding of their mind or will to what the government proposes.

Does that sound like real life to you? Do you agree with whatever the government makes you do? Have you yielded your mind to paying as much taxes as you're required to, for example?

Obviously, every person disagrees with at least one thing the state does, right? To address this *dis*agreement, advocates of the state have conjured up all sorts of arguments in an attempt to circumvent the clear language of the Declaration. First, they argue against explicit consent—the idea that to agree to something, *you actually have to personally agree.* Explicit consent is when you yourself verbally say yes or sign a written contract. If you download software and accept the terms and conditions, you explicitly consented. If you sign an employment contract, you gave explicit consent to do what your employer is requiring of you. When you buy lemonade from a child working at a roadside stand, you explicitly consent to pay the stated amount in exchange for the drink.

Good luck getting 100% of the state's subjects to agree to its every action. Because this is impossible, advocates then argue that explicit consent is not required. *Implied* consent, they say, is sufficient. This is the idea that *you don't actually have to personally agree* in order to... agree. This is an assumption of permission based on a person's behavior. A typical example of implied consent is finding an unconscious person who needs CPR performed. That person has not given you permission to place your mouth on theirs or perform chest compressions, but you assume that if they *were* able to verbally agree, they *would*, so you proceed with that implied consent.

But what about conscious people who don't consent—those of us who are able to agree verbally or in writing, but do not? This is where things start to break down. Based on a person's behavior, advocates of the state find creative ways to argue that he has given the government implied consent to do whatever it does. Let's explore a few of these arguments and demonstrate why they do not constitute consent.

"If you don't like it, leave!"

Perhaps the most commonly used assertion is that residency constitutes implied consent for the state. This argument says that if you choose to live or remain in a certain location, you are agreeing to be subject to the various forms of government that claim jurisdiction over that area. Sounds like the gang territory example, right?

The key problem with this argument is it assumes that the authority is legitimate—that the state has the right to do what it wants within the territory over which it claims power. Telling somebody "if you don't like it, leave" completely sidesteps a discussion about whether the state's mandates are legitimate at all.

It's also unreasonable to suggest that a person has to relocate in order to refuse consent. Not everybody can move, of course. Elderly folks may become less mobile over time. Sick people need their medical team. Some homeowners can't find a buyer for their house. Others might want to leave, but simply have nowhere else to go. Do these people—none of whom are able to leave—consent to be ruled as the state wishes? Remember Webster's definition, and the question becomes clearer: have these individuals yielded their mind in agreement?

Let's imagine a liberal Democrat—we'll call him Joe—who lives in one of the most conservative areas of the country in order to take care of his sister who suffers from a rare disease and cannot function without another person's support. Will Joe agree with what the government in his neck of the woods is doing? Probably not. Has he yielded his mind? Not likely. And yet, because he lives in that territory, he is subject to the state. And based on where he finds it necessary to live, many would argue that he has given implied consent to the conservative-dominated government.

Let's consider another scenario. Imagine a single mother who, after having a hard time finding employment, finally lands a job so she can provide for her children. At this job, her boss begins to make unwanted advances toward her. The woman, now a victim, finds it necessary to continue working with him so she can feed her children, worried what will happen if she reports him, and that if she were to quit, she wouldn't find another job.

Has she consented to these unwanted advances? Absolutely not. She has not agreed; she has not yielded her mind in unity with her boss. Her behavior—continuing to show up for work—cannot be taken as implied consent by the boss. Her choice to remain in his presence is a calculation she makes for other reasons, not because she wants her boss to continue his inappropriate actions.

People choose to live where they do for many reasons. Perhaps the property has been in the family for generations, or a person has specialized in a specific set of tasks for which there are few employers, which reduces the options of where that person can live. Maybe there are medical reasons for someone to remain close to a certain hospital or a need to live near an ailing relative who requires care. These choices are independent of any consideration about the state itself; a person's decision regarding where to live cannot be interpreted as consent.

Just as the single mother continued working for her boss despite his conduct, people choose to continue living in a certain location not because they consent to gangs or governments that claim the territory, but because—all things considered—that's where they want or need to live. Residency does not constitute consent.

"You voted, now accept the outcome!"

Another common argument you'll hear in support of implied consent is that voting creates consent. Participating in the state's processes, many say, implies you agree with its operations; if you vote, then you must accept the outcome of that vote.

Imagine Candidate Moore is running for office, hoping to gain control of political power in the area where you live. You like this guy and would consent to have him in charge. Unfortunately, he was defeated by Candidate Rodriguez, who is now in a position to pass laws that control your life. You disagree with Rodriguez very strongly and do not consent to him having power over you. Does your agreement with Moore constitute agreement to be governed by whoever might beat him in an election?

Now let's imagine that the candidate you liked actually won—Candidate Moore became Congressman Moore. But he lied through his teeth, saying things on the campaign trail that sounded good; now that he's in power, he's ruthless. He sponsors legislation that would negatively affect your family's business, and you clearly disagree with what he's doing. You may have consented to his efforts initially, but now you find yourself disagreeing substantially. You do not consent to be governed by Moore and the product of his legislative efforts—even though you voted for him!

The argument that voting establishes consent breaks down even more when you consider how elections actually work. Yes, sometimes people will strongly support the candidate or policy they are voting for. But quite often people are choosing a "lesser of two evils," opting to pick the person they dislike least. This isn't consent, just as it isn't consent to prefer one gang's occupation of your neighborhood compared to its rival.

Lysander Spooner put it this way:

> In truth, in the case of individuals, their actual voting is not to be taken as proof of consent, even for the time being. On the contrary, it is to be considered that, without his consent having even been asked a man finds himself environed by a government that he cannot resist; a government that forces him to pay money, render service, and forego the exercise of many of his natural rights, under peril of weighty punishments. He sees, too, that other men practice this tyranny over him by the use of the ballot. He sees further, that, if he will but use the ballot himself, he has some chance of relieving himself from this tyranny of others, by subjecting them to his own.[20]

What he's saying here is that many people treat voting as a calculated effort by which they can try to reduce the negative impact of the state. Trying to minimize bad things in government by voting for the preferable option does not imply that the individual agrees with anything—he merely wants to shield himself.

Spooner continues, observing that "if he uses the ballot, he may become a master; if he does not use it, he must become a slave." A person is compelled either to vote to control others (in an effort, ideally, to get them to respect his natural rights), or be controlled. "He has no other alternative than these two," Spooner argues, noting that a person's decision to vote effectively becomes "self-defense." He continues:

> His case is analogous to that of a man who has been forced into battle, where he must either kill others, or be killed himself. Because, to save his own life in battle, a man takes the lives of his opponents, it is not to be inferred that the battle is one of his own choosing. Neither in contests with the ballot—which is a mere substitute for a bullet—because, as his only chance of self-preservation, a man uses a ballot, is it to be inferred that the contest is one into which he voluntarily entered; that he voluntarily set up all his own natural rights, as a stake against those of others, to be lost or won by the mere power of numbers.[21]

As you recall, consent is a yielding of the mind—an agreement. Does the liberal Democrat in a conservative area yield their mind by showing up each year to vote for the minority candidate who clearly won't win, but with whom they agree? Does a man yield his mind to an oppressive government that is ruining his family's business merely because, in vain, he helps campaign for a losing cause that a majority of people will not support?

As Spooner argued, the behavior of casting a vote does not convey enough information to know if a person is actually yielding their mind. For all we know, they imagine themselves in a political battlefield and are merely trying to preserve their life, liberty, and property, hoping to dodge the political bullets being fired at them through the ballot box. For these reasons, voting does not constitute consent.

"Speak now or forever hold your peace!"

In previous arguments we have discussed certain behaviors that some believe create implied consent for the state. In this argument, it's not an action that is interpreted as consent, but the lack thereof—specifically, remaining silent.

"Silence is consent" has permeated our culture as a saying people will sometimes use. For example, a business executive on a conference call might propose an action plan to which nobody responds—perhaps the proposal is stunning in its awfulness, or perhaps the executive is an intimidating figure nobody dares to challenge. "Silence is consent," he might say in reply, reaffirming that if nobody speaks up, he's going to move forward with the plan. But did these individuals yield their mind?

Imagine that one of your neighbors painted their garage door bright pink. Everybody in the area might hate it and worry that it will negatively affect the property value of their own homes. But nobody says anything, for fear of causing conflict. That neighbor, receiving no negative input on his choice of color, then interprets that silence as suggesting that everybody in the neighborhood must be okay with it. But they're not—they just haven't spoken up to directly indicate their disagreement. It's no surprise that they haven't yielded their minds because *inside* their minds they're thinking, "That guy is crazy!"

There are numerous reasons why a person might choose silence over speaking out in cases where they disagree—especially since the government has guns and is willing to use them. Throughout world history, people have lived under despotic regimes but chosen to remain passive and compliant—not because they like what's happening, but because they are terrified by the consequences of actively objecting.

And let's be clear on one thing: the state wants to punish dissent so others are not encouraged to act likewise. This creates even more of a disincentive for those who dissent to speak out—they don't want to be made "an example" by attracting retaliation.

Consider the case of Irwin Schiff, a longtime tax protester who believed that the U.S. income tax was invalid and did not apply to him as the Internal Revenue Service claimed. On many occasions he refused to pay the tax, resulting in years of unsuccessful court battles. Sentenced to nearly 13 years in prison at age 78 for his *malum prohibitum* crime, Schiff—who had become legally blind and was dying of cancer—died at age 87, shackled to a hospital bed in a guarded room.[22]

Imagine what would happen if the government validated the claims of a tax protester? Millions would immediately pursue the same course of action. The government opted to act decisively, and the warning to others was clear: if you don't like paying taxes, don't speak out about it and attract attention that might bring you the same fate.

This argument of silence creating consent really breaks down when you think of those, like Schiff, who *do* speak out. If a person explicitly manifests their dissent, are they exempt from the state's authority? If silence does create consent, then surely those who are not silent can free themselves from this power by speaking out, right? Of course not. Silence does not constitute consent.

"But you're doing what they tell you!"

The final argument we'll address is the one that is used the least—and it's basically another version of the silence argument we just discussed. Some suggest that obedience to the state's mandates is a form of implied consent, in that there is behavior to indicate that a person is agreeing to do what they are told—else why would they do it?

Since we just refuted the "silence is consent" argument, you can probably dispense with this one fairly easily as well. The same response applies: going through the motions does not mean that a person has yielded their mind. We do all sorts of things for fear of the consequences of *not* doing them—observing the speed limit, paying taxes, or even securing a permit to operate a lemonade stand.

Viktor Frankl was an Austrian psychiatrist born to a Jewish family—a circumstance that led to his imprisonment in the Auschwitz concentration camp in 1944.

As you might imagine, this environment was oppressive and dehumanizing. Forced labor, poor (if any) food, and state-sponsored murder were part of the awful routine. Prisoners like Frankl— as would be expected in such a scenario—did what they were told; the prisoners obeyed. But these outward acts did not reflect their inner beliefs and desires, as he explained:

Viktor Frankl

> Every day, every hour, offered the opportunity to make a decision, a decision which determined whether you would or would not submit to those powers which threatened to rob you of your very self, your inner freedom; which determined whether or not you would become the plaything of circumstance, renouncing freedom and dignity to become molded into the form of the typical inmate.[23]

As a psychiatrist, Frankl focused on preserving, and even increasing, his inner self and spirituality—even in circumstances in which it seemed few options existed to do so. Even while obeying, Frankl and his fellow prisoners were maintaining their views and, of course, not yielding their minds. They did not agree; they did not consent.

Randy Barnett, a constitutional professor and author, points out the key problem with this argument:

> Does one really manifest a consent to obey the commands of someone much more powerful simply because one does not physically resist the threat of violence for noncompliance?[24]

Just as failing to speak out does not create consent, deciding not to actively resist and fight back does not mean that a person has yielded their mind in agreement. Obedience does not constitute consent.

Consent matters—in our businesses, intimate relationships, and our voluntary associations. We expect explicit consent to be the standard; we do not work for an employer who hasn't agreed to hire us, or initiate intimacy with a person who has not agreed, or force people to associate with us if they don't want to. This is common practice and widely understood.

Why, then, do we expect a *lower* standard from the state, especially since its activities involve applying unnatural consequences—fining, imprisoning, and even killing people? If explicit consent is the standard for society, then why are we letting the state off the hook?

In our voluntary relationships, consent has meaning because people are free to *dissent* if they so choose. You cannot yield your mind in agreement if there is not a meaningful opportunity to *disagree*. You can refuse to work for a boss you don't like; you can get out of an intimate relationship that becomes toxic; you can leave the local park cleanup club if you prefer to spend your time elsewhere. These voluntary relationships matter because those involved *voluntarily* signal their desire to remain together by not dissenting. This is how and why their consent has meaning.

But the state does not tolerate dissent. You are governed whether you like it or not. And so, while the Declaration of Independence says the state derives its "just powers" from the consent of the governed, we respond that no such consent exists in our day. Neither residency, nor voting, nor silence, nor our obedience constitutes consent—not even implied consent, let alone explicit consent.

If the state does not—indeed, *cannot*—have the consent of those it governs, then how can *any* government legitimately exist?

AWAY WITH THE STATE

Barnett explains, "Consent must be real, not fictional—unanimous not majoritarian. Anything less than unanimous consent simply cannot bind non-consenting persons."[25] Most people immediately respond: is there *any* government that has unanimous consent? That idea sounds absurd! It'll never happen!

Well, it does happen in a variety of governments. This is where it becomes important to refer to our earlier distinction between *government* and the *state*. We defined the "state" as a type of political organization that uses coercion and claims authority over a specific territory. When most people say "government," they are actually referring to the state. But there are governments that have unanimous consent. They just aren't "states" because they don't match the two criteria.

Your family has a government. So does your church. Businesses have them, too. Even the local PTA and Boy Scout chapters have governments. And all those associations Tocqueville saw? Each of them had their own government as well. Governance becomes necessary when large groups of people interact, in order to establish rules by which the organization will operate. Everybody agrees to the terms, and those who disagree can disassociate themselves if they wish.

The state forces those within its jurisdiction to associate with it. The community choir, on the other hand, does not compel you to join; you are not subject to its government unless you want to be. The state is tied to a geography, whereas voluntary government knows no bounds unless those involved want it to be tied to a geography—for example, a sports team. The state does not allow people to opt out, whereas in other governments people may leave if they wish. The state binds everybody, including future generations as people are born within its territory. But if you agree to work for a company, that company is not entitled to the labor of your children as well—your consent is yours alone.

Most importantly, as Barnett indicated was necessary, these voluntary associations *actually have the consent of those who participate*. There are no mind games being played to conjure up implied consent; if you suddenly grow to hate chess, your former chess mates will not tie you to a chair and force you to continue playing with them.

How could a political government ever function like voluntary associations do? Think of your neighbors; while you may get along with one another nicely, it's likely you belong to different groups. You might belong to a different church, attend different schools, use a different internet service provider, root for different sports teams, and work with different charitable groups. The fact that you live next to one another does not compel you to share these things in common; you remain free to associate with those you wish to.

So why must neighbors be forced to associate in the same political government? Why must the conservative Republican in the most socialist part of the country be compelled to be subject to the same government as those with whom he strongly disagrees? Can't these governments abide by the same principles as other organizations? Why do we treat the state any differently? If anything, shouldn't we be *more* demanding of consent and legitimacy since political governments tend to be a touch more violent than the chess club or Boy Scouts?

Society functions as a result of the market—an exchange of ideas, products, and services in which those who want our money or time are competing against one another. The local insurance agent knows that if his prices are too high, you'll go elsewhere. Don't like the offerings from the restaurant down the road? Your family will keep driving to find something better. And if the book club is causing you grief, you might search out another like-minded group—or better yet, start your own!

Mobility is important in this competition. Without having to disrupt your life by moving elsewhere, you can choose from a variety of organizations with which you might affiliate. And because it's easy for you to leave one and join another, these organizations have an interest in constantly trying to win you over—they have an incentive to be on their best behavior. They improve their quality, lower their prices, and increase their attention to customer service. If they don't, they'll lose your support—and if others join you, they will go out of business.

Monopolies don't share these characteristics. Think of the United States Postal Service. It's well known for being inefficient and slow, with poor customer service, ever-increasing prices, and an inability to reap a profit. Congress prohibited competition with the USPS for delivering letters, punishable by a fine of up to $500, a six-month stint in prison, or both. And it's exempt from state and local taxes, a $14 billion per year boost that UPS and FedEx don't enjoy.

Remember Lysander Spooner, the essayist from earlier in the chapter? He tried to compete against the USPS. Frustrated by declining quality of service and increasing costs, he set up the American Letter Mail Company, both to provide a better service and to directly challenge the government-created postal monopoly. USPS revenue began to decline as Spooner's company grew.

One of Spooner's stamps

In response, the Postmaster General convinced Congress to lower the price of mail—something set not naturally by the market, but artificially by the government itself. In March 1845, the reduction in price was legally approved. Spooner, in turn, lowered *his* rates to keep up the competition. A few years later, Congress fired back, lowering the rates again while also enacting a new law to further protect the government's monopoly on mail distribution—closing the remaining loophole Spooner was using. He was defeated—put out of business by the state.[26] And since that time, prices have exploded while service continues to be substandard. This is the danger of not having competition.

The same feelings many have for the USPS are the same as what they feel toward the state itself. Without any options to choose from, we reluctantly go along with the scheme, hoping for something better. We grow frustrated with the increasing costs and declining quality—especially while seeing the wonders competition brings to other areas of our life like food production, technology, communications, and more.

What would political governments be like if they were subjected to competition? For starters, you could affiliate with the political government of your choosing. Just as you can pick from different cable companies or fitness centers, you would be able to select which protection services (the basic function of government) you wanted. Of course, some governments might cost more due to offering services beyond protection: trash collection, health insurance, business certification, etc. Without having to uproot your family and move to an unfamiliar location, you could change affiliations—you could dissent by disassociating. And this competition would inevitably increase the quality and decrease the cost of government.

And the cost? Taxation under the state is theft. We begrudge it, even if some of it is going to helpful things, because much of it is not. And as taxes continue to increase, we grow more frustrated in our quiet dissent. (Few of us are willing to protest as Irwin Schiff did.) But under a form of political government that involves consent and competition within the same territory, taxes would change into a mere membership fee. Because you would be explicitly consenting to a government and the services it is offering, you would therefore be agreeing to the terms of that affiliation. Just as you might pay a membership fee for the local fitness center or online education program (each of which has governments, remember), you'd be paying a fee to the political government of your choosing.

No longer would people grumble so much about laws they didn't like—there would be terms and conditions to which they yielded their mind. And if they didn't like them, the barrier to disassociation would be convenient and feasible, unlike today where you'd have to uproot your entire life in search for a different state which, let's be honest, would likely have many of the same problems as the one where you currently live.

Imagine you're a business owner whose competition is quickly gaining on you. You're losing customers because of your competitor's more attractive offerings and better price options. This is a *signal*—information that helps you refine your approach and hopefully win back some of those lost customers. States don't receive these signals because it's extremely unrealistic that many people would either revolt or relocate. And even if they did, as with any monopoly, this information would neither be transmitted to nor welcomed by those in charge. They have no incentive to respond to complaints and concerns. But if it were easy to disassociate from a political government, that valuable information would incentivize the leaders of the abandoned government to improve.

Most importantly, the government would actually have "the consent of the governed" without having to play mind games to justify it. If Barnett's right, and legitimate government must have unanimous consent to be binding on those it governs, then this structure is the only one I can imagine that will allow everybody to yield their mind as they please; the state must be subject to the same market forces as society. In effect, *there can be no more state*, since its very nature requires a territorial monopoly. It would have to simply become a political service organization that affects only its members who consent to its governance. What a different world that would be!

Much of the world's history involves political governments that did not have the consent of their subjects. We're not used to this idea, and it's difficult to imagine it working because it seems so... unfamiliar. But whether it's been tried before or not is beside the point—what matters is finding an arrangement in which the lofty aspiration of the Declaration of Independence is actually realized. We who create organizations also create political governments—just as in our island example. We who comprise society must oppose the existence of the state because it is impossible for a monopoly to have unanimous consent. If we desire a legitimate political government, we should demand nothing less.

NOTES

1. Brian Rosebury, *Tolkien: A Cultural Phenomenon* (New York: Palgrave Macmillan, 2003), 178.
2. Graham Chapman et. al, "Repression is Nine Tenths of the Law?," *Monty Python and the Holy Grail*, directed by Terry Gilliam and Terry Jones (Culver City, CA: Columbia Tristar Home Entertainment, 2001).
3. Bastiat, *The Law*, 3.
4. Ross Harrison, "Jeremy Bentham," in *The Oxford Companion to Philosophy* (Oxford: Oxford University Press, 1995), 85–88.
5. Jeremy Bentham, *An Introduction to the Principles of Morals and Legislation* (Mineola, NY: Dover Publications, 2007), 5.
6. John Austin, *Lectures on Jurisprudence, Or, The Philosophy of Positive Law* (New York: Henry Holt & Co., 1875), 105.
7. Frederick Pollock, *The History of English Law Before the Time of Edward I*, ed. Frederic William Maitland (Cambridge, MA: Harvard University Press, 1899), 515-518.
8. William Blackstone, *The Political Text Book; Comprising a View of the Origin and Objects of Government* (London: William Strange, 1833), 111.
9. Hamilton et. al, *The Federalist on The New Constitution*, 374.
10. Jonathan Elliot, ed., *The Debates in the Several State Conventions on the Adoption of the Federal Constitution*, vol. 3 (Washington, DC: Jonathan Elliot, 1836), 533.
11. Ibid, 555.
12. Alexis de Tocqueville, *Democracy in America*, vol. 2 (Cambridge: Sever & Francis, 1862), 129.
13. Ibid, 130.
14. Murray Rothbard, *Anatomy of the State* (Auburn, AL: Ludwig von Mises Institute, 2009), 11.

15. Rothbard, *Anatomy of the State*, 15.

16. Bastiat, *The Law*, 26.

17. Ibid.

18. Tocqueville, *Democracy in America*, 134

19. *Webster's Dictionary*, 1829 ed., s.v. "consent," http://webstersdictionary1828.com/Dictionary/consent.

20. Lysander Spooner, *No Treason No. II: The Constitution* (Boston: Lysander Spooner, 1867), 5-6.

21. Ibid, 6.

22. "Death of a Patriot," Peter Schiff Podcast, October 17, 2015, http://www.schiffradio.com/death-of-a-patriot/.

23. Viktor Frankl, *Man's Search for Meaning* (New York City: Washington Square, 1984),87.

24. Randy Barnett, *Restoring the Lost Constitution: The Presumption of Liberty* (Princeton: Princeton University Press, 2004), 21.

25. Ibid, 11.

26. "Lysander Spooner and the United States Postal Monopoly," Digital Journal, April 18, 2009, http://www.digitaljournal.com/article/271139.

"The most foolish notion of all is the belief that everything is just which is found in the customs or laws of nations. Would that be true, even if these laws had been enacted by tyrants?"[1]

Cicero

CIVIL DISOBEDIENCE

Equality 7-2521 is the identity given to the main character in *Anthem*, a short novel by Ayn Rand. This person, stripped of any individuality, lives in a future dark age where children are raised apart from their families, overseen by the Council of Eugenics. There is no freedom or individual liberty, only "the great WE, One, indivisible and forever."

The protagonist aspires to science and scholarship, but this hope is in vain; the Council of Vocations chooses each person's profession. Equality 7-2521 is to be a Street Sweeper. This is how he is expected to contribute to the collective. But he is not prone to obey his masters without questions; Equality 7-2521 is born with what he calls a "curse" of curiosity—he learns quickly and asks questions.

This curiosity is nurtured when, in a tunnel, he finds signs of the distant past—the "Unmentionable Times" from a fallen society when things were different. Equality 7-2521 begins sneaking away to conduct science experiments—an action that is forbidden because it is done without approval. He rediscovers electricity and thinks his scientific success surely will be well received by the World Council of Scholars. But alas, they criticize him as a "gutter cleaner," ordering that he be punished and his experiment destroyed, lest its discovery negatively affect the Department of Candles.

Equality 7-2521 defies the Council and flees, learning on his own to rediscover what freedom is. Embracing his newfound individuality, and struggling to understand its implications, he finally realizes that "centuries of chains and lashes will not kill the spirit of man nor the sense of truth within him."[2]

Anthem is a work of dystopian fiction—a genre that describes a future time of oppression. The protagonists in this type of novel are typically rebels who disobey the abusive authorities and try to disrupt their plans. We cheer them on with each page, hoping their resistance succeeds so they can be liberated and enjoy peace and prosperity. And the stories are very popular. Consider

Hunger Games, wherein Katniss Everdeen becomes the face of the rebellion, fighting against President Snow's Panem. Katniss and other Tributes collaborate in their disobedience and actively work to undermine the Capitol's efforts to maintain its ruthless stranglehold over the districts. Then there's *Star Wars*, the franchise that popularized rebellion against imperialism, inviting the audience to cheer on a group of dissidents.

These stories are not fantasy; the issues presented are not alien to our world. Instead, we recognize in these stories our observations and experiences about the real world. We sympathize with the protagonists because we see their suffering at the hands of the state. We revere their bravery and wonder what it would be like to be in their shoes. Part of us might be jealous of their opportunity to actively oppose the oppression they face, while we instead silently suffer.

Thomas Jefferson and his fellow contributors to the Declaration of Independence knew that such opposition is rare. "Mankind are more disposed to suffer," they wrote, "than to right themselves by abolishing the forms [of the state] to which they are accustomed." But their story is similar, and it wasn't fiction. The colonists who rebelled against the most powerful empire on Earth basically became a real-life *Star Wars* story, two centuries before the movie was filmed. Rebels smuggled illegal goods, refused to pay certain taxes, settled land they weren't allowed to, tarred and feathered tax collectors, destroyed tea at Boston Harbor in protest of a government-granted monopoly, and more. And when the Crown cracked down on the colonies, these rebels stood their ground and fought back. What's more, the Americans fully seceded from British rule, disassociating themselves from its government and refusing to recognize its authority over them. Essentially, they blew up the Death Star.

The history of our world is one of illegitimate governments oppressing people, requiring heavy taxes, causing wars, and interfering in the everyday affairs of their subjects. And while examples of inspiring opposition—major or minor—are few and far between, those that do happen are worth sharing and studying. These stories feature individuals who, in essence, do not break any moral law, but instead oppose a man-made *malum prohibitum* that is in conflict with their natural rights. Think of a homeowner who is in possession of a shotgun, which his state has forbidden, who uses the illegal weapon to successfully repel an invader. Or consider the case of cancer patients who use cannabis to soothe their pain and increase their appetite, even though the state threatens to put them in prison and remove their children from their home if they're caught.

In cases such as these, civil disobedience, as these acts are commonly called, is really *obedience* to a higher moral law. And like the other issues of law, this one has a Latin expression: *lex injusta non est lex* ("an unjust law is not a law"). People may disregard a mandate the state says they must obey when that mandate is in conflict with a higher law the person chooses to follow. Are such people justified?

Yes, according to Henry David Thoreau, a philosopher and author who spent two years living a social experiment at Walden Pond, on property owned by his friend Ralph Waldo Emerson near Concord,   Massachusetts. One year into his project (trying to "live deliberately"

Henry David Thoreau

and escape "over-civilization"), the local tax collector confronted Thoreau and demanded he pay the six years of poll taxes he owed and had failed to pay. Thoreau refused, believing that this tax was helping to fund the Mexican-American war and the expansion of slavery, both of which he strongly opposed. Thoreau was arrested and put in jail; an unidentified woman paid his debt, though the tax collector kept him locked up overnight.[3]

"Must the citizen... resign his conscience to the legislator?" Thoreau asked in "Civil Disobedience," an essay he wrote about the experience. "Why has every man a conscience then? I think that we should be men first, and subjects afterward." He was emphatic that issues of moral importance should not be suppressed merely because a majority of legislators have passed a law ordering it. "It is not desirable to cultivate a respect for the law," he added, "so much as for the right."[4] To Thoreau, laws were only worthy of respect and allegiance when they did not violate one's conscience—when they were right or, in other words, when laws do not violate our natural rights.

Thoreau's provocative essay explores this question in detail and has served as inspiration for a wide range of individuals engaging in civil disobedience, from Gandhi and Martin Luther King Jr., to Vietnam War protesters in America and pro-democracy protesters in Tiananmen Square, China. Ask yourself: what should you do when you are ordered to do something you feel is morally wrong? Is a person required to submit to the state in all cases whatsoever? Using the language of this book, are you responsible to forever obey a state that does not have the consent of the governed and that utilizes positive law to enact all sorts of *malum prohibitum* mandates that wrongly restrict your freedom?

When doing the right thing has been made wrong by the state, you will find yourself in quite an awkward position—one that many people shy away from, silently doing what they are told, fearing the consequences of disobedience to the state. That's natural and understandable. But those who choose to dissent when their actions are morally justified have an opportunity to educate a great number of people who see and sympathize with their actions. Do you recall Arnold Abbott, who fed the homeless despite being arrested by the police and ordered by city officials to stop? Millions of people throughout the world saw the news of his actions and cheered him on, bringing so much shame upon the state that its agents were pressured into leaving him alone. And every time a child's lemonade stand is shut down for failure to obtain a government permission slip, parents everywhere shake their heads at the unreasonable silliness of the bureaucrats and police officers who are giving that child a personal education in the very lessons this book discusses.

History has provided us other examples to which we can look for inspiration and emulation—courageous people who stood up against the state to choose the right, when right was deemed to be wrong. Let's look at a few stories.

WILLIAM PENN

William Penn

Have you ever been to Pennsylvania or studied American history? If so, chances are that you were taught that that state was given its name in honor of the colony's founder, William Penn. This man, a Quaker, is well known to many as an early supporter of confederacy between the colonies. But his most impressive stories come from decades before, as a youthful activist and advocate of religious freedom in England.

Born to a militaristic father and a socialite mother, Penn soon found he didn't quite fit in his own family. Sent to study at Oxford, young Penn was expelled for criticizing the Church of England and rebelling against forced worship. Furious over his expulsion, his father attacked him with a cane and kicked him out of their home, denying him any future inheritance.

Now homeless, Penn found shelter in the homes of some Quaker families. This religion and lifestyle slowly began to appeal to young Penn. Perhaps he was impressed by their refusal to bow or take off their hats to any superiors, believing that all men were equal before God—an idea that was quite contrary to the concept of the monarchy in England. Quakers, then, were treated as heretics—religious rebels—because of their principles and their refusal to swear oaths of loyalty to the king.

At the time, the government in England effectively prohibited minority religions in an effort to shut down competition—especially the disruptive type. Quakers were basically denied the ability to freely worship, and Penn was arrested for attending one of their meetings. Rather than denying he was a Quaker to escape legal consequences, he publicly declared himself a member, formally joining their ranks at the age of 22.

In 1668, and at the age of 24, Penn wrote his first pamphlet, *Truth Exalted: To Princes, Priests and People*, a criticism of all religious groups other than Quakers. In it, for example, he called the Catholic Church the "Whore of Babylon," and he didn't have nice things to say about the official Church of England, either.[5]

In the same year, Penn authored *Sandy Foundation Shaken*, which attacked the doctrine of the Trinity (the nature of the Father, the Son, and the Holy Ghost). Penn's barbed writings were controversial and triggered an open rebuke by some clergy in the Church of England—especially the Bishop of London, where the pamphlets were printed and circulated. This Bishop secured an order of imprisonment for William, who was to be locked up indefinitely until he publicly recanted his remarks. Penn was placed in solitary confinement in an unheated cell, threatened with a life sentence for saying what he did about his religious beliefs. While the real "crime" the state was punishing was blasphemy—a punishable crime when church and state are tied together—Penn was officially charged with "publication without a license."

How would you have responded in such a circumstance? At what point do you compromise your beliefs in order to be safe and avoid punishment? What do you do when your conscience says one thing but the state says another?

Penn was resolute; he refused to submit. The "prison shall be my grave before I will budge a jot, for I owe my conscience to no mortal man,"[6] he said. He petitioned the king for an audience—it was the king himself who signed the warrant putting Penn in prison—but was denied. After eight months, he was finally released. Liberated from captivity, many in Penn's shoes would seek the shadows, hoping to avoid any future altercations. Most people prefer to go on living their lives, but not Penn, who committed to continuing his fight against the Church and the Crown.

It was not easy to be a Quaker in England during Penn's time. Their refusal to recognize authority and active preaching of a different doctrine were met with hostility, and numerous laws were passed that allowed for the arrest and persecution of Quakers. Dozens had died in prison, and countless others were crippled or made sick through maltreatment; thousands of them were imprisoned for their religious beliefs. Quakers were whipped, publicly humiliated, stripped naked, fined, and had their property confiscated.

Penn himself was arrested several times on charges of illegal preaching and "inciting a riot"—code for discussing things the government doesn't like. And these instances weren't accidental or unwelcome. In fact, Penn directly provoked one of the laws in order to challenge it. The 1664 Conventicle Act prohibited the gathering of "more than five persons... for any religious purpose not according to the rules of the Church of England."[7] In effect, this prohibition outlawed religious meetings of, and preaching by, any who had nonconformist religious views, such as the Quakers.

In 1670, Penn and another Quaker, William Mead, preached their faith to an assembled crowd of around 300 outside Grace Church in London. The jury in Penn's resulting court case refused to convict him— even though they had been instructed to come to a de-

William Penn's trial

cision without hearing Penn's defense of his actions.
Many jurors felt strongly about the injustice of the law
itself. They returned a verdict of guilt only in "speaking at Grace Church," which was not itself illegal. The
panel of judges was furious, leading the presiding judge
to tell the jury:

> Gentlemen, you shall not be dismissed until we
> have a verdict that the court will accept; and
> you shall be locked up without meat, drink, fire,
> or tobacco. You shall not think thus to abuse
> the court. We will have a verdict by the help of
> God, or you shall starve for it.[8]

The judges repeatedly sequestered the jury, and once denied them food and water, in hopes of a different result, but each time the same verdict was rendered for the alleged crime: *not guilty*. Finally, in frustration at the jury's defiance, the judges put Penn in jail and the entire jury was forced to join him—each of whom was fined nearly a year's wages for going against the court's wishes.

While Penn was sitting in jail once again, his father was dying. Penn wanted to see his father in hopes of reconciling their rocky relationship, but encouraged him, in a letter, "not to purchase my liberty" by paying the fine. But his father refused, probably worried he might not see his son before dying, and Penn was released. Interestingly, the jurors fought their unjust imprisonment and won a legal challenge that created a judicial precedent (or rule) that has remained in place ever since, including in America: juries are independent of the court and cannot be punished for their decision. Penn's provocation of the law, and his stubborn defense of his rights, has protected religious liberty and the independence of the jury for millions who followed him.

This hero, later a founding father, was not content to submit; he did not passively accept the "rule of law." He recognized a wrong and fought against it, being willing to openly violate the unjust mandate in order to legally challenge it. Penn wasn't trying to quietly break the law for his own gain, sneaking around to avoid detection—he used civil disobedience as a vehicle to educate the masses and put the tyranny of church and state on display for all to see.

He even won over his father. Having now gained some respect for Penn's integrity and courage, he told his son in a letter, "Let nothing in this world tempt you to wrong your conscience."[9]

A decade later in America, Penn began drafting a charter of liberties for the newly settled land he was given under a charter from the king to settle a debt with his father and provide a place where Quakers could emigrate in order to reduce tensions in England. Not surprisingly, this charter guaranteed a fair trial by jury, freedom of religion, and freedom from unjust imprisonment.

HELMUTH HÜBENER

As a young boy in Germany during the mid-1900s, Helmuth Hübener joined the local scouting chapter of the Boy Scouts—an organization supported by the Mormon church to which he belonged. As it was an international organization, the rising regime of the National Socialist German Workers' Party, the "Nazis,"

eventually prohibited par-
ticipation within the country. Hitler Youth activities
became mandatory instead.

Having grown up in a
dysfunctional family that
was not political, young
Helmuth was not inherently
opposed to what he encoun-
tered in the Hitler Youth.

Helmuth Hübener

According to one of his best friends, he "was quite en-
thused at the beginning," though another friend sug-
gests that Helmuth's apparent support for the program
was to "put up a smoke screen so others would not see
his real convictions."[10] We will never know and can
only speculate. Why? Because Helmuth was executed
by the Nazi state—beheaded in prison—at the age of
17. He was the youngest enemy of the Third Reich to
be sentenced to death and executed.

Helmuth's negative opinion of the Nazis developed
due to personal observations of what was occurring in
his community. For example, one friend recalls a con-
frontation in the street with a Hitler Youth patrol as
Helmuth and his buddies were singing some American songs. The uniformed youth stopped the boys, demanding to know why they were singing those songs.

"Why shouldn't we sing them?" Helmuth said. "It's not against the law! Talking about the law, what right do you have to harass German citizens on the street? You've not been given the authority of a policeman to question people!"[11] The Hitler Youth group backed down and departed, but Helmuth wasn't finished sounding off about what had happened:

> That's the trouble with these people—put them in a uniform and they think they have the authority to bully people around.... Our country is being run through threats, intimidation, and even brutal force! And something has to be done about this![12]

On September 1, 1939, Germany started World War II by invading Poland. On the same day, Nazi Propaganda Minister Joseph Goebbels announced the "Extraordinary Radio Measures" decree. Anyone caught listening to a foreign radio station would be put in prison, and distributing information derived from foreign broadcasts was made punishable by death. To satisfy the public's desire for information about the war, the Nazis mass-produced inexpensive radio receivers with a short reception range and only a few channels—ones controlled by the state. Germans called one of the models the *Goebbels-Schnauze*, or Goebbels's snout.

But Helmuth wanted real information, and he knew that he wouldn't get it from domestic sources. So, he committed the only real crime of his short life by breaking into a locked cabinet in his grandparents' apartment to retrieve a more powerful radio belonging to his half-brother who was away fighting in the war. Helmuth, 16 years old at the time, invited his friends over to join him. The group of young men listened intently, riveted by the information they were hearing from forbidden sources. And for Helmuth's part, he was quickly convinced that what he was hearing was truthful. As one example, the British Broadcasting Corporation's updates would list the losses of British troops, aircraft, and ships, while the Nazis never shared information of their weakness or defeat with German citizens, presumably in an effort to appear strong and victorious—to keep up a charade, deceiving the public.

Passive listening quickly turned to active resistance—after all, Helmuth felt "something has to be done." The teenager began illegally producing leaflets that appeared to be imprinted with an official Nazi Party stamp. One was titled *Down with Hitler* and, rather than calling Hitler the *Volksführer* ("people's leader"), he used *Volksverführer*, the people's seducer. Helmuth also called Hitler the "people's corruptor" and the

Hübener, center, with his friends and accomplices

"people's traitor."[13] One of his friends shared how they began spreading Helmuth's leaflets:

> He gave me a handbill, about one quarter of the size of a sheet of typing paper, and asked me to read it. Entitled, "Hitler the Murderer," ... I told him the pamphlet looked great, particularly because it was printed on red paper. "Then let's go to work," Helmuth replied. He handed me a stack of leaflets and said, "Put them in mailboxes, telephone booths, and other places—be inventive." I went [to an apartment building] and began dropping off the handbills in the

> mailboxes... I covered about three apartment
> houses before my supply ran out. I distributed
> about thirty to thirty-five handbills that night.[14]

To some it may have appeared that the youthful rebels considered this a sort of adrenaline-fueled
game. One of Helmuth's friends noted "the excitement
of doing something secretive," a feeling similar to one
they experienced years prior when the group worked
together as a made-up "Lord Lister Detective Agency"
to ascertain the guilt of people whose stories they read
in the paper. But for Helmuth, this resistance was serious business: he wanted to start a revolution. For several months, he and his two friends carried out a propaganda campaign against the establishment, hoping to
distribute enough contradictory information that their
fellow Germans would help oppose the Nazis.

Based on the Gestapo's archive, Helmuth wrote
29 pamphlets, sometimes with different audiences in
mind. For example, in one that targeted members of
the Hitler Youth after the announcement of a new,
severe disciplinary policy for any insubordination,
Helmuth wrote the following:

> So this is the Hitler Youth, praised far and wide.
> A compulsory organization of the first order
> for recruiting Nazi-enslaved national comrades.
> Hitler and his accomplices know that they must

> deprive you of your free will at the beginning,
> in order to make submissive, spineless creatures
> out of you... "You are the future of Germany,"
> they will tell you, but then you are tyrannized
> and punished for any little offense.[15]

Can you imagine yourself, at age 16, writing such material and going to such great lengths to distribute it? Even more surprisingly, despite his friends growing increasingly nervous about their efforts, Helmuth never showed any signs of fear. He knew there was work to be done.

He didn't succeed. Nine years of the Nazi regime's rule, and two years of war, produced indifference—not activism—among the German population. Helmuth and his friends may have reached a sympathetic few, but there was never any uprising. Their effort came to a halt when, in an effort to expand their ranks by soliciting help from other teens, they were overheard and caught. The Gestapo arrested Helmuth Hübener.

Along with other subversives, Helmuth and his friends would be tried for their supposed crimes before the infamous People's Court. This court was sometimes referred to as the "Blood Tribunal" because around 90% of the cases heard before the court during the final years of Nazi rule resulted in a death sentence or life imprisonment.[16] Set up outside of the country's constitutional framework as a "special court"—Hitler unilaterally created it after being displeased with the results of the regular court of law—the ruling judge often acted as the prosecutor, criticized defendants, and pronounced his verdict and the sentence without the defendant even speaking.

A group that tried to assassinate Hitler was brought before this court, and when the high-profile participants tried to mount a defense, they were shouted down or forced to shut up. In contrast, young 17-year-old Helmuth had no public significance or standing, but he refused to be silenced. His friends, awaiting their fate, recall their friend and leader standing up to the President Judge and shouting, "You have sentenced me to death for telling the truth. My time is now—but your time will come!"

While his friends were sentenced to a few years in prison, allowing them to survive the war and live to an old age, Helmuth was declared guilty of conspiracy to commit high treason against the Third Reich. It was very unusual for the Nazis to prosecute an underage defendant such as Helmuth, but the court argued that the young rebel had shown more than average intelligence for a boy of his age.

In addition to being sentenced to death, Helmuth was also stripped of his civil rights, enabling his captors to mistreat him in prison. He was denied bedding and blankets in a cold cell, where he awaited his fate for two months. A red poster announcing his fate, written in large black writing, was posted in public to announce the scheduled beheading—a warning to the local population against following in the young man's footsteps.

The sole surviving letter Helmuth wrote from prison was to a fellow church member. "I know that God lives and He will be the Just Judge in this matter," Helmuth wrote on the day of his death. "I look forward to seeing you in a better world!"[17]

ROSA PARKS

Rosa Parks

Following her parents' separation in 1915, Rosa McCauley spent much of her childhood on her grandparent's farm in Alabama with her brother. Born into a family of African descent, Rosa remembers being adversely affected by the Jim Crow laws implemented in southern states—government mandates that separated white people from black people in much of their daily lives. Public restrooms, drinking fountains, schools, transportation—these and other daily doings were racially split, and the divisions were enforced by law.

Rosa recalls gaining the understanding at age six that black people like her were "actually not free." One memory she shared in her autobiography illustrates how her grandfather reacted to the Ku Klux Klan—a violent group of white supremacists:

> At one point the violence was so bad that my grandfather kept his gun—a double barreled shotgun—close by at all times. And I remember we talked about how just in case the Klansmen broke into our house, we should go to bed with our clothes on so we would be ready to run if we had to. I remember my grandfather saying, "I don't know how long I would last if they came breaking in here, but I'm getting the first one who comes through the door."[18]

Even from a young age, Rosa had developed a defiant streak. When she was around 10 years old, a white boy insulted and threatened to punch her. She picked up a brick and dared him to hit her. Not surprisingly, the boy opted to leave her alone. On another occasion, a white boy on roller skates purposefully bumped into her, hoping to knock her off a sidewalk. She turned around and pushed him, resulting in the boy's mother, who saw the altercation, threatening to have young Rosa arrested and jailed for pushing her son. Rosa, who had a strong sense of fairness and justice, wouldn't stand for that—she forcefully objected, pointing out that she had not bothered the boy before being pushed by him.[19]

Both schools and the transportation methods to get the children to them were segregated. Rosa lived near a white school but was required to walk a greater distance to the Mount Zion AME Church, where she and about 60 other black students were taught in a one-room schoolhouse by a single teacher. The white children had a new brick schoolhouse, paid for by taxpayers, that was fully heated and featured separate rooms and teachers for each grade level. White children were given a bus to ride; black children had to walk. And as the bus passed the black kids heading to school, the white ones would sometimes throw trash at them.[20]

This racial separation continued throughout much of Rosa's adult life, especially after she married Raymond Parks, a barber who was active in Civil Rights movement. Now known as Rosa Parks, she joined the National Association for the Advancement of Colored People and became secretary to the organization's president. Rosa began working at the Maxwell Air Force Base in 1944—a federally owned facility in which segregation was not allowed. This was Rosa's first time experiencing equality between blacks and whites, and it changed her. "You might just say Maxwell opened my eyes up," she later recalled.[21]

A decade later, fatigued from the effects of legalized racism every single day in her community, Rosa invoked the defiant attitude of her youth to deal with the injustice that faced her on a bus ride home from work on December 1, 1955. At the time, black people were required to sit in the back seats to allow whites to sit up front. The seats allocated for whites were full, so the driver moved the "colored" sign back one row to free up four more seats for white passengers.

Rosa was sitting in that row of seats. The three other black passengers moved, but Rosa did not. The driver asked her why she wasn't standing up, to which she replied, "I don't think I should have to stand up." This resistance—both to established law and cultural practice—was thought by some in later years to be a result of Rosa merely being too tired to get up and move. "That isn't true," she wrote in her autobiography. "I was not tired physically... No, the only tired I was, was tired of giving in."[22]

Two police officers approached the stopped bus and, after reviewing the situation, arrested Rosa for her refusal to cooperate with the law. "Why do you push us around?" she asked one of the officers. He replied: "I don't know, but the law's the law."[23] Rosa was booked into jail and briefly incarcerated. She was allowed to call her husband, but by then word of her arrest had quickly spread. A civil rights activist named E.D. Nixon heard about her arrest and was waiting for Rosa later that evening when she was released. For several years, Nixon had been trying to find a courageous black person who was honest and of good character to become the plaintiff in a court case to challenge the constitutionality of segregation laws. That day, he had found his plaintiff in Rosa Parks.[24]

Four days later, during her trial, Nixon and his allies organized a boycott of all buses in Montgomery, Alabama. Tens of thousands of fliers had been circulated announcing the plans, and when Rosa Parks was found guilty of violating the segregation laws and fined $14, African-Americans in her community stood in solidarity with her. Nixon and some local pastors used the momentum from the boycott to form the Montgomery Improvement Association. A new arrival in town, a reverend just 26 years old, was elected as the organization's president. His name was Martin Luther King Jr.[25]

Rosa Parks's case was appealed all the way to the U.S. Supreme Court. While that process unfolded, the bus boycott angered many white people in the city, and there was some violence—the homes of both Nixon and King were bombed. But the activists pressed forward, creating substantial press coverage and ultimately a victory from the Supreme Court. Rosa Parks became "the mother of the civil rights movement."

Parks suffered in her later years—both financially and physically. Despite these trials, she was honored throughout her life for her role in sparking a movement and endearing many to the cause of equal rights. Looking back on her actions, she wrote:

> The time had just come when I had been pushed as far as I could stand to be pushed, I suppose... I had decided that I would have to know, once and for all, what rights I had as a human being, and a citizen.[26]

Rosa's civil disobedience created a long chain of events that helped bring the answer to that very question.

Parks riding a bus following the U.S. Supreme Court decision

...AND MANY MORE

In 1971, a massive "non-cooperation" movement was launched against the ruling government in West Pakistan in order to pressure the Pakistani state to accept the results of the previous year's election. Government offices, public transportation, and schools all shut down as East Pakistanis stopped paying their taxes. The civil disobedience ended when the Pakistan Army launched a military offensive 18 days later, killing tens of thousands.[27]

Egyptians chafed under British rule in the early 1900s. Saad Zaghloul worked with fellow activists to rally the people towards independence, using acts of civil disobedience to frustrate Britain's efforts to maintain its authority. Ministers quit and lawyers went on strike, bringing the judicial system to a halt. Trade guilds, religious leaders, and students demonstrated in the streets against the Brits. Fearing an uprising, British authorities arrested Zaghloul and exiled him from the country. But the acts of civil disobedience continued, leading in several instances to revolutionary violence. The opposition forced London to issue a declaration of Egyptian independence in 1922. Now free, Zaghloul became Egypt's first popularly elected Prime Minister in 1924.[28]

Following the state-sponsored execution of Jesus Christ, his apostles had continued preaching their Christian doctrine—something that the Jews saw as heretical and worthy of punishment. The Sadducees, a Jewish sect that dominated the government, had presumably hoped that killing Jesus would stop the uprising and force his followers to disperse. This didn't happen, so the authorities, who by this point were "filled with indignation," ordered the arrest and imprisonment of Peter and his fellow apostles. They were released without permission overnight—the Bible says it was an angel's doing—and resumed preaching. Arrested once more, the apostles were brought before the high priest who said, "Did not we straitly command you that ye should not teach in this name? and, behold, ye have filled Jerusalem with your doctrine, and intend to bring this man's blood upon us." Peter's response was simple, and points to the virtue of civil disobedience in following a higher law that conflicts with an unjust, man-made law: "We ought to obey God rather than men."[29] The apostles were physically beaten and then released.

Along with other men his age, boxing legend Muhammad Ali was called up in the draft to enlist in the army. Ali, who had been a longtime opponent of the Vietnam War, showed up to the Houston Military Entrance Processing Station in Texas. As each man's name was called out, he stepped forward to begin the induction process. Ali refused to comply, for which he was arrested, and was then tried, convicted, and sentenced to five years in prison for refusing to serve in the military. He was also ordered to pay a $10,000 fine for draft evasion. Ali explained his defiance: "Why should me and other so-called 'negroes' go 10,000 miles away from home, here in America, to drop bombs and bullets on other innocent brown people who's never bothered us? I will say directly: No, I will not go."[30] His principled stance cost him dearly. Though the U.S. Supreme Court overturned his conviction a few years later, Ali was stripped of his world heavyweight title, and his boxing license was suspended.[31]

And, as you can guess, civil disobedience can even apply to a simple lemonade stand. After seeing news reports of little children having their stands shut down by police officers and bureaucrats, Robert Fernandes created "Lemonade Freedom Day" to raise awareness of the problem and, as an adult, practice some civil disobedience to show the injustice of the law. "These kids are learning how to run a small business," Fernandes said. "I think by telling them they can't do that, you're shutting down their dreams." Fernandes and a group of other protesters set up shop on the front lawn of the U.S. Capitol, joined in protest by others around the country doing the same thing in their various locations. Police officers arrived, ordering them to leave. "So you want to be arrested for your cause of lemonade liberation?" one officer taunted. As dozens of cups of lemonade were distributed for ten cents apiece, three of the participants were arrested for "vending without a permit."[32]

Day after day, thousands of positive laws turn otherwise law-abiding individuals into criminals for doing nothing wrong. Peaceful acts of civil disobedience, when done in furtherance of a higher law, can help others realize the injustice an individual faces and rally support to push for change. Open defiance for the right reasons, and handled in the right way, can inspire others to act; it's hard to see a person suffering unjustly without having a desire to help.

If there are so many positive laws prohibiting things that aren't inherently wrong, why don't we see *more* civil disobedience? If thousands of unjust laws restrict the rights of billions of people, why aren't there enough stories of resistance to fill entire libraries? The answer is rather simple: risk tolerance.

In the financial world, risk tolerance is a basic method used to determine how you want to save or invest the money you've earned. If you want to play it safe and avoid losing your money, then you can put it in a savings account at the bank. If you're willing to risk losing your money with the potential of earning a lot more if things go well, then maybe you would buy a company's stock or invest in a mutual fund.

This same situation applies to doing what the state requires of you. It may be unjust and illegitimate, but each person must make a calculation about how much risk they are willing to assume. If the issue is unimportant—for example, jaywalking—then it may not be worth having to pay a large fine or having to tell future employers that you have an arrest record. But if the issue is significant—for example, the National Security Agency spying on American citizens without first obtaining a warrant—then it may be worth risking your freedoms in order to alert the public and push for legal reform.

Jefferson and his fellow Declaration drafters were right: "all experience hath shewn [*sic*] that mankind are more disposed to suffer, while evils are sufferable, than to right themselves by abolishing [or, perhaps, resisting] the forms to which they are accustomed." History offers us inspiring stories of those who chose to stand up for what's right when it was declared wrong. But many people prefer to avoid risk and play it safe—and that's understandable. There are many reasons to resist, and anyone who has not given the state consent should, in theory at least, *dissent*. But we generally don't because we prefer to remain with our family rather than in a jail cell. Liberty isn't easy, after all.

After Thoreau was freed from jail, he set out to continue his social experiment. Children in the nearby area asked for his help searching for huckleberries in a nearby field. Thoreau enjoyed the experience—he was in nature, living. As he walked along one of the town's highest hills, presumably soaking in the surrounding sights, he looked around and observed that "the state was nowhere to be seen."[33] Others may try to control our lives unjustly, and we may struggle under the burdens the state places upon us. But the world of Equality 7-2521 is fortunately not ours—we still have and understand our individuality. The state is not everywhere, nor can it control everything—and we should act accordingly. That's all civil disobedience is.

NOTES

1. Micheline Ishay, ed., *The Human Rights Reader: Major Political Writings, Essays, Speeches, and Documents from the Bible to the Present* (New York: Routledge, 1997) 26.
2. See Ayn Rand, *Anthem* (Claremont; Coyote Canyon Press, 2008).
3. Harold Bloom, ed., *Henry David Thoreau* (New York: Bloom's, 2008), 6.
4. Henry David Thoreau, "Civil Disobedience" (Salt Lake City: Libertas Institute, 2014), 3.
5. J. Sowle, ed., *A Collection of the Works of William Penn* (London: J. Sowle, 1726), 241
6. Mary Maples Dunn and Richard S. Dunn, eds., *The Papers of William Penn*, vol. 1: 1644-1679 (Philadelphia: University of Pennsylvania Press, 1981), 85.
7. John D. Inazu, *Liberty's Refuge: The Forgotten Freedom of Assembly* (New Haven: Yale University Press, 2012), 24.
8. Charles F. Partington, ed., *The British Cyclopedia of Biography*, vol. 2 (London: WM. S. ORR & Co. 1838), 558.
9. Thomas Clarkson, ed., *Memoirs of the Private and Public Life of William Penn*, vol. 1 (Dover: Samuel Stevens, 1827), 39.
10. David Conley Nelson, *Moroni and the Swastika: Mormons in Nazi Germany* (Norman, OK: University of Oklahoma Press, 2015), 290.
11. Ibid, 292.
12. Ibid.
13. Ibid, 297.
14. Ibid, 298.
15. Ibid, 303.
16. Peter Wyden, *The Hitler Virus* (New York: Arcade Publishing, 2002).

17. Paul R. Bartrop, *Resisting the Holocaust: Upstanders, Partisans, and Survivors* (Santa Barbara: ABC-CLIO, 2016), 105.

18. Joyce A. Hanson, *Rosa Parks: A Biography* (Santa Barbara: Greenwood, 2011), 10.

19. Ibid, 11.

20. Ibid.

21. Rosa Parks, *Rosa Parks: My Story* (New York: Puffin Books, 1999), 142.

22. Ibid, 116.

23. Ibid, 117.

24. "Rosa Parks," History, http://www.history.com/topics/black-history/rosa-parks.

25. Ibid.

26. Stewart Burns, *Daybreak of Freedom: The Montgomery Bus Boycott* (Chapel Hill: University of North Carolina Press, 1997) 83-84.

27. See S.M. Shamsul Alam, *Governmentality and Counter-Hegemony in Bangladesh* (New York: Palgrave Macmillan, 2015).

28. M. Cherif Bassiouni, *Chronicles of the Egyptian Revolution and Its Aftermath: 2011–2016* (New York: Cambridge University Press, 2017), 571.

29. Acts 5:17-28.

30. Tom Mulle, "Muhammad Ali Was No Draft Dodger," *Newsweek*, June 6, 2016, http://www.newsweek.com/muhammad-ali-was-no-draft-dodger-466955.

31. "Muhammad Ali Was Stripped of His World Heavyweight Title for Refusing to Join the Army in 1967," *New York Daily News*, June 3, 2016, http://www.nydailynews.com/sports/ali-stripped-title-refusing-join-army-1967-article-1.2660321.

32. Alexander Abad-Santos, "The Battle Against Lemonade Stand Crackdowns," *Atlantic*, August 22, 2011, https://www.theatlantic.com/business/archive/2011/08/battle-agasint-lemonade-stand-crackdowns/354415/.

33. Thoreau, "Civil Disobedience," 24.

CONCLUSION

Lemonade stands may be a staple of summertime, but they are also an excellent analogy for the modern clash between freedom and the state. Sure, it may be easy to simply comply—to pay the money and pass the inspections and get the permission slip—but whatever happened to simply having some fun and making some money without all the bureaucracy and red tape? Whatever happened to having freedom?

If one thing should be clear by this point in the book, it's this: true freedom is not something that is experienced in today's world. States rule without the consent of the governed; positive laws abound. There are many laws that can easily be classified as immoral or unjust, and there may be times when you are compelled to do something that violates your conscience. The state's success depends upon *your* submission.

"There may be times when we are powerless to prevent injustice," observed Elie Wiesel, winner of the Nobel Peace Prize in 1986, during his acceptance speech. "But there must never be a time when we fail to protest."[1] These words have power because they are deeply personal. At age 15, Wiesel watched as German soldiers invaded his Hungarian town, deporting his family alongside the other Jews to Auschwitz, where up to 90% of the people who were imprisoned there were exterminated. His mother and younger sister were immediately murdered, while he and his father were forced to perform manual labor until they could no longer do so, at which point they would also be killed in the gas chambers. His father was later beaten and killed; Wiesel survived, carrying the tattoo of his inmate number on his left arm for the rest of his life as a reminder of the oppression he experienced.[2]

Acts of tyranny such as these are fortunately rare. It is not common to experience such awful displays of state-sponsored aggression. Rather, most violations of one's natural rights are simple, quiet, and far less controversial. Think of the mother who does African hair braiding, only to be shut down by the state for failure to obtain a cosmetology license—one that requires 2,000 hours of training at a school that doesn't even teach African hair braiding. What about an Uber driver who is fined thousands of dollars because the city's laws prohibit this form of transportation in an effort to protect taxis? Then there are the senior citizens whose lawns begin drying up who then receive warnings and fines from city bureaucrats for having an unsightly landscape. Or, consider the plight of an unemployed property owner who loses his home after being arrested for renting out his basement so he could have enough money to pay his mortgage.

These violations are akin to the ancient Chinese strategy of *lingchi*. Throughout history, the state has been one of the leading causes of death; in the twentieth century alone, 262 million people worldwide were killed *by their own government*.[3] Known as democide, the methods used to kill nonconformist citizens are typically quick: bombs, guns, gas, etc. But in imperial China, *lingchi* was often used—a slow form of torture sometimes called "death by a thousand cuts." Those sentenced to this fate would be tied to a post, and repeatedly cut until death finally came sometime later. This is the form in which most threats to our freedom appear—small, slow, and simple. For example, the government is likely not going to seize your bank account and take all your money. Instead, you'll simply be told to pay your ever-increasing taxes, bit by bit, year after year.

This is heavy stuff, no doubt. You may be unsure what to do about any of this. The problems seem so large, and the ideal seems so far off, that you wonder what can be done—if anything.

What if I told you that you have already done something that will help?

Imagine for a moment that you own a piece of land—one that has been in your family's possession for a very long time. But this land is in dispute because a neighbor claims that some of it is actually his. The problem is, you're not sure if he's right or not—you don't know quite where the boundaries of your land are. Through the generations, some legal documents about your property were lost, and others had handwriting that was hard to interpret. So the neighbor, seeing your uncertainty, begins to encroach further and further onto the land. You suspect he has gone too far, but because you're not sure where the property line actually is, you can't stop him.

If you can't point and say, "You may not go past this line," then *there is no line*. You can't defend what you don't know to be true.

If you don't understand what types of law are valid, then you would be led to assume that all of them are. If you can't identify a *malum prohibitum*, your sense of right and wrong will be blurry; you could not point out that something is considered wrong merely because some politicians declare it so. And if you are unaware of the problems of implied consent, then you can't comprehend why the state's authority over you is illegitimate.

If you don't know what your rights are, you are powerless to protect them as your neighbors, through the state, encroach upon them further and further. But you *do* know, so you can try to protect them. You now have a line to point to. *There is a line.*

What you do with this information is up to you. Perhaps you'll be a more informed voter. Maybe you'll start a nonprofit organization to educate others or become a political science professor to help the rising generation understand this line. You might seek an elected office to try and repeal *malum prohibitum* laws. Maybe you'll simply go about your business, finding the huckleberry fields in your own life where the state is nowhere to be seen.

Or maybe you'll set up a lemonade stand—without anyone's permission.

NOTES

1. Elie Wiesel, "Hope, Despair and Memory," Nobel Lecture, December 11, 1986, http://www.nobelprize.org/nobel_prizes/peace/laureates/1986/wiesel-lecture.html.
2. Elie Wiesel, *Night* (New York City: Hill and Wang, 2006).
3. R. J. Rummel, *Death by Government* (New Brunswick: Transaction Publishers, 1994).

AUTHOR'S NOTE

While Henry David Thoreau advocated for civil disobedience in certain cases, he posed a question that each of us must answer:

> Unjust laws exist; shall we be content to obey them, or shall we endeavor to amend them, and obey them until we have succeeded, or shall we transgress them at once?[1]

Elaine Augustine, like most parents, wants her children to be law-abiding citizens. But the laws requiring her children to obtain permits and licenses and pay fees to the government in order to set up shop from time to time are wrong. She faced the same question Thoreau posed. "Here was a ridiculous law leaving me the option of ignoring it and teaching my kids that it was okay to ignore the law," she said, "or, voluntarily complying by either making my children get licensed or not letting them engage in business activities."[2]

Elaine decided to educate her children about the law and "engage them in the process of changing it." For four years, the organization I lead, Libertas Institute, had been advocating for an amendment to the law in our home state of Utah that would exempt home-based businesses from licenses and fees. During each year's legislative session, Elaine would testify in support of the bill alongside several of her children, who would explain why they felt the licensure laws were unreasonable. We repeatedly lost, facing opposition from lobbyists representing the cities and counties who benefitted from all the fee revenue small business owners were required to pay.

On our fourth try, we finally won—the bill passed the Utah Legislature and was signed into law. Even better, we made a last-minute change that made the proposal even better: children under the age of 18 would no longer be required to obtain any business licenses, health inspection permits, or pay fees to the government. For them, in Utah, there is now a free market.

Here is the language that we settled on:

> A municipality may not require a license or permit for a business that is operated:
>
> (i) only occasionally; and
>
> (ii) by an individual who is under 18 years of age;

That's it. Lemonade stands in one state were liberated through this simple amendment. And while plenty of renegade lemonade stands were previously operating in Utah year after year, now they are fully compliant, since an unjust law was amended away into oblivion—the state's power was limited.

It's not always that easy; the state does not easily relinquish its power. Political efforts take some time and are often unsuccessful. But in case you'd like to try, consider looking up who your state representative and senator are and asking them to sponsor legislation that does the same. Tell them that Utah has led the way, and you'd like your state to follow. And if you'd like an organizational ally like Elaine had in Libertas Institute, find your state's free market think tank on the map at the State Policy Network website: SPN.org. Tell them Libertas Institute sent you their way.

Good luck!

NOTES

1. Thoreau, "Civil Disobedience," 12.
2. "The Libertas Institute Makes Sure Kids Keep Their Lemonade Stands in Utah," Atlas Network, June 23, 2017, https://www.atlasnetwork.org/news/article/the-libertas-institute-makes-sure-kids-keep-their-lemonade-stands-in-utah.

RECOMMENDED READING

Intrigued by what you read about in this book? Here is a brief list, in no particular order, of important political, economic, and philosophical books that will expand your knowledge and help you better understand the ideas introduced in *Lessons from a Lemonade Stand*. Many of these books can be found for free online.

- Frédéric Bastiat, *The Law* — This essay, written in 1850 by a French political economist, serves as a great introduction to understanding what true laws are and should be. Bastiat's writing is especially enjoyable because of his wit and sarcasm used to attack false ideas.

- Auberon Herbert, *The Right and Wrong of Compulsion* — Herbert briefly served in Parliament in England, but quickly became frustrated with the status quo. He formed the Party of Individual Liberty to advocate for "thorough" individualism and this essay, written in 1885, was the party's manifesto making the case for voluntaryism.

- Henry Hazlitt, *Economics in One Lesson* — Because an understanding of economics is essential to comprehend law and moral order, this book is helpful to introduce core concepts to the reader who may be unfamiliar with economic theory. Written in 1946 while Hazlitt worked for the *New York Times*, the book is a persuasive rebuttal to many popular, destructive economic fallacies.

- Murray Rothbard, *Anatomy of the State* —As a brief essay, this quick read makes a concise case for why the state is a predatory entity that increases in size and strength at our expense. An economist and historian, Rothbard published this powerful essay in 1974 to expose the state's true nature and pinpoint the main problem underlying a history of conquest and carnage by governments around the world.

- Ron Paul, *Liberty Defined* — Why did people of such differing sociopolitical backgrounds join together in support of two presidential campaigns for former congressman Ron Paul? The candidate addresses that question in a comprehensive case for liberty in this book, demonstrating the non-partisan and widespread appeal of taking a principled stance on the issues.

- Ayn Rand, *Atlas Shrugged* — Using fiction to demonstrate the power of ideas, Rand portrays a society in which socialism cannibalizes and alienates the innovators whose contributions are needed and without whom society begins to fall apart. This book is especially helpful in visualizing the effects that laws have on the market.

- Murray Rothbard, *For a New Liberty* — Readers who are persuaded or intrigued by *Lessons from a Lemonade Stand* will find in Rothbard a deeper and broader inquiry into the basis of law and the case for eliminating the state. Written in 1973, this is an engaging read in which Rothbard aims to explain and defend libertarianism.

- F.A. Hayek, *The Constitution of Liberty* — This book is the result of four decades of study and thought on the nature of economic, political, and social interactions, and the possibility of a free society. Hayek, a Nobel-prize winning economist, wrote this book in 1960 to explain and defend the importance and impact of freedom.

INDEX

ABOUT THE AUTHOR

Connor Boyack is president of Libertas Institute, a free market think tank in Utah. In that capacity, he has spearheaded a number of successful policy reforms in areas such as education reform, civil liberties, government transparency, business deregulation, personal freedom, and more.

Connor is also president of The Association for Teaching Kids Economics, a nationally focused non-profit training teachers on basic economic principles so they are empowered and motivated to help their students learn more about the free market.

A public speaker and author of over a dozen books, Connor is best known for The Tuttle Twins books, a children's series introducing young readers to economic, political, and civic principles.

Connor lives near Salt Lake City, Utah, with his wife and two homeschooled children.

Find Boyack's books for sale at LibertasUtah.org/shop/